SKILFUL
SOCCER

Peter Treadwell

A & C Black · London

First published 1991 by
A & C Black (Publishers) Ltd
35 Bedford Row, London WC1R 4JH

ISBN 0 7136 3254 2

A CIP catalogue record for this book is available from
the British Library.

Acknowledgements

Thanks to the staff and students at the Cardiff
Institute of Higher Education for their help and
advice and especially to my demonstrators,
Frank, Rob, Simon, Steve and the two Richards,
to photographer Ron Hardacre and to chief
librarian Lyndon Pugh. Thanks also to Neil
Sutton who was responsible for preparing all of
the line drawings in this book.

Typeset by Latimer Trend & Company Ltd,
Plymouth, Devon.
Printed and bound in Great Britain by
William Clowes Ltd, Beccles and London.

CONTENTS

INTRODUCTION

The game of soccer holds a special place in British popular culture for a whole variety of reasons. One of these reasons is that the game regularly produces individuals of sparkling genius and unbridled talent, who play with a mixture of technical mastery, personality (charisma) and athleticism. Some people argue that supreme skill is innate and, to a certain extent, that may be true. However, just like any profession in any walk of life, these skills also can be learned. Good coaching is about providing countless opportunities to develop individual skill so that players of all ages can utilise their talents.

To be able to perform well at any level in soccer, the player has to learn a range of skills which must be practised and refined continually. Also, players should maximise their opportunities for learning new skills since exposure to technical practice is vital whatever their age. A good coach should have in his mind, or better still on paper, a repertoire of those skills that are essential for effective performance in any soccer position. While we can all think of players who have done particularly well in professional soccer even though they only possess a few technical skills, for example at heading or tackling, players and coaches should aim for complete technical mastery of soccer skills. In the following chapters, I will be identifying the essential skills both on and off the ball and showing how they can be practised in relative technical isolation or in pressurised game-like situations.

To develop soccer technique players must possess or acquire the ability to perform isolated physical activities. These activities are learned by doing or 'feeling' the action or, sometimes, by watching and listening to a 'master' performance or demonstration. Either way, sound soccer technique development should include constant repetition of practices and allow the player sufficient time on the ball.

However, at some stage individual technical efficiency or high level mastery (as demonstrated by many South American ball jugglers over the years) has to be placed in a wider context, that is the game situation. In this environment the ball juggler may not be such a skilful footballer, because as well as carrying out physical on-the-ball activities he also has to pay attention to the surrounding football environment in order to select the appropriate technique. The player then enters into a decision making process, affected by variables such as his position in relation to the opposition and his own team-mates, and this lends a certain degree of unpredictability to the game.

Techniques only become skills when they are utilised in a particular playing environment, whether that is a full game, a conditioned game, or a small-sided game. Successful coaching means that a player is able to transfer those essential isolated techniques into the open, competitive environment of the match. Thus playing skills, and coaching skills for that matter, are acquired through a process, and can only be honed to perfection over a period of time.

It has been said that soccer coaching at the present time concentrates too much on physical conditioning as opposed to technical training. I would go further than that and suggest that soccer currently caters for both of these aspects of training pretty poorly. Coaches are not knowledgeable enough about the physiology of performance and yet they still pay lip service to it in their training sessions, to the detriment of individual technique and skill development. Players must take responsibility for their own fitness development outside of squad or team sessions, when individual and team skills ought to have priority. Individuals can only excel if they have a rich reservoir of skills to draw upon, and teams can only be successful if they foster a combination of individual creativity and structured unit play. The best teams never sacrifice individuality, but instead blend it into their team play and allow it to blossom.

PLAYING POSITIONS

The goalkeeper

Clearly the goalkeeper has a set role which is specific to him alone. He must control his area and successfully deal with shots and crosses. Also, he must be able to advise defenders as to their positioning, being the overall 'marshall' in defensive situations. Furthermore, when his team regains possession from a broken-down attack, he is the initiator of any new attacking move. It is worth noting that any team must have an outfield player who is able to stand in for the keeper should any injury occur.

The striker

As the name implies, the striker is invariably the team's main strike-force at goal, and the principle target for any long passes into the opposition's defence. The striker should be a clinical finisher on both feet, and should possess a range of heading, shielding and dribbling skills. Quite often the striker performs a lonely role, battling with his back to the central defenders, attempting to turn and take opponents on, or holding up the ball and waiting for support.

Midfield players

These players are the point of contact between defence and attack. They exist as part of a unit, often having particular roles like ball-winner or play-maker, or having a 'free' role in which they attempt to encompass every aspect of midfield play. Midfield players are required literally to go wherever the ball is, and so they are primarily concerned with covering space and making ground. They endeavour to be on the ball as much as possible, and they attempt to dictate play. As such, midfield players are often the key decision-makers in a team, trying to take the correct passing options and controlling the flow of the match.

The defender

Like the midfield player, the defender is part of a unit which is likely to consist of two wide defenders (usually the full backs) and two central defenders. (These names obviously refer to the area of the pitch they are required to patrol.) Their main task is to thwart any attacks in these parts of the pitch, both on the ground and in the air. If they win the ball, defenders usually release it to midfield with a quick pass. Because of their position, it is not often a good idea to dribble the ball out of defence. Therefore accuracy is vital both for long and short passing, as is their ability to win the ball.

One particular type of defender, the sweeper (who plays either behind or sometimes just in front of his central defenders), has to have every skill imaginable, for he is seen as the final outfield defender, the play-maker and occasionally the attacker all rolled into one. He will mark the essential space around his defenders, depending upon where the ball is, and it is not an uncommon sight to see this type of player bringing the ball out of his own area and creating an instant attack.

Other positions

Other clearly defined roles sometimes exist for players, notably the wide receiver or winger. The traditional winger's role would be to hug the flanks and literally fetch and carry the ball along the wing before attempting to get in a telling cross. However, in modern football certain midfield and wide defenders individually or collectively perform this role.

Possibly the main point to make about playing positions is that young players should have experience of them all so that they can learn the relevant game strategies. Some roles require very specific skills, and youngsters should learn via the game situation what these are.

ON-THE-BALL SKILLS

Every footballer loves to have the ball under control at his feet so that he is dictating play. It is essential to recognise this fact when teaching new techniques to players of all ages. Successful coaching is about making players technically competent, so that when they are in possession in a game they feel confident and able to utilise that possession to maximum effect. Only then can tactical awareness be introduced. Of course the coach cannot totally control match tactics, but by promoting basic skills he can, together with his players, dictate the structure and function of technique practices. In matches the coach stays in the 'dug out' and can only hope that the game follows an agreed plan or strategy.

Thus while the coach can expose his players to unit practices which will prepare them, to a certain extent, for actual matches, nothing can belie the fact that his central concern should be to promote essential soccer skills. The only drawback to the coach's promotion of technique is the inability of young players to attend to, and take in, great amounts of soccer information. With both young and adult footballers, the coach should place the emphasis on developing technical efficiency but relate that training as soon as is appropriate to the game situation.

It is important, therefore, to place the central focus on individual technical advancement, instead of rushing towards game-like practices without paying sufficient attention to the player's readiness to enter the competitive environment. To that end, this section begins with what all players desire most, that is mastery and control of the ball.

The following drills offer a particular structure for training skills which centres around providing:

- technical information
- coaching advice and feedback
- actual practices.

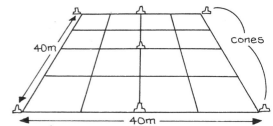

Fig. A   A gridded area for use in coaching. The 16 units are capable of holding between 30 and 48 players

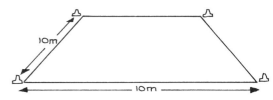

Fig. B   An individual grid for 2–4 players

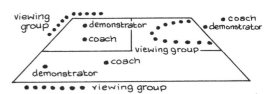

Fig. C   Possible demonstration patterns

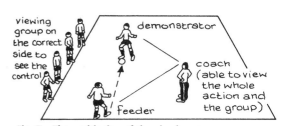

Fig. D   The positioning of the viewing group

Running with and dribbling the ball

Running with the ball provides the soccer player with a tremendous opportunity for displaying and demonstrating his individual skills. However, it is often said that the highly structured modern game thwarts the emergence of great on-the-ball virtuosi.

Technical information

1. Keep the ball under control at a convenient distance in front of your feet, so that it is readily obtainable if a defender closes in and also so that you can run at pace and stop and move direction at will.
2. Generate a slight forward body lean.
3. Bend at the knees a little so as to lower your body's centre of gravity and thus facilitate easy pivoting movements.

Controlling the ball along a line. Note the player's concentration on the ball and his good body position

Coaching advice to the player

1. Attend to the ball *and* the immediate area beyond and around it.
2. Run with the ball confidently.

Objectives

1. To encourage running with the ball.
2. To develop control and peripheral vision on the ball.

Drills

Players run with the ball under control:

- up and down a gridded 'corridor'
- diagonally across a corridor
- sideways across a corridor
- at random
- with 'controlled' opposition.

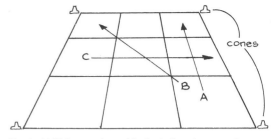

Fig. 1   Drill for running with the ball under control

These practices should be carried out separately at first, then collectively, and finally with controlled and conditioned opposition.

Advanced on-the-ball techniques

The following individual ball technique practices can either follow on directly after the previous exercise or be held jointly within those initial drills in a full session. The practices still take place without opposition, or have opposition of a controlled kind. The basic principle behind these drills is that the player seeks to gain control over the ball, utilising a variety of full and part-body movements.

Technical information

1. Concentrate on and immediately around the ball.
2. Use all surfaces of the foot to control and move the ball, notably the inside, the outside, the heel and the sole.

Outside of the foot control when running with the ball

Coaching advice to the player

1. Try to emphasise 'quick feet', i.e. working in contact with the ball at speed.
2. Take controlled strides and get up on your feet, that is off your heels, when moving.
3. Try to relax and search for a rhythm in your movement.
4. Gradually build up to your maximum running speed on the ball.

Objective

To encourage the development of more advanced dribbling skills.

Drill 1

■ Carry the ball forwards with the inside of the feet into open space.
■ Place a controlling foot inside the ball.
■ Lean forwards.
■ Sink slightly at the hips.
■ With your weight on the outside foot, move away with the ball in a different direction.

If you repeat the drill alternating the feet, then a zig-zag movement is created.

Fig. 2   Drill 1

Drill 2

■ Guide the ball with the instep then stop it with the sole of your boot.
■ Check and momentarily adopt a more upright body position.
■ Dip and move away again in the same direction, occasionally alternating your foot control.

This drill can be performed in the single grid or in open space.

Drill 3

■ As with drill 2, but this time after stopping the ball move away to the left or the right.

Drill 4

■ As with drill 2, but after stopping the ball, lift or scoop it away to the left or the right by using the outside of the foot (as if to raise the ball over an imaginary tackler's leg).

Drill 5

■ Guide the ball forwards for a few yards and let it run ahead.
■ Go after the ball and run beyond it slightly.
■ Backheel the ball, pivot quickly and return.

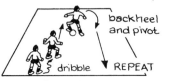

Fig. 3   Drills 5 and 6

Drill 6

As with drill 5, but this time instead of backheeling the ball, step beyond it and drag the ball back behind you with the inside of the non-pivoting foot.

Drill 7

■ Position the ball immediately in front of you and adopt a slightly more upright stance.
■ Experiment by dragging the ball across and around you using the sole of the boot.
■ The action of the foot is to move on, across and down on the ball.

Players can practise these individual technique drills on their own, and this should be encouraged by giving players a ball each to take home with them, or by advising them to buy their own match football or cheap, heavy-duty, plastic ball. What should be stressed is the need to get these techniques individualised and perfected. Once this has happened, then the player, in his own time, can adapt and refine existing techniques and also begin to compose new techniques. There are a great many more ball techniques than are shown here; those covered are just a few that relate to using different parts of the foot for control.

Group practices

The following section contains group practices to be learned under the supervision of the coach.

Drill 1 – running forwards

- Exert control with the inside and outside of both feet.
- As you get beyond half-way, look ahead so that you hear or see any command of 'Stop' from the coach.

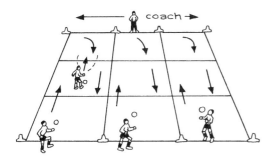

Fig. 4   Drill 1 – running forwards

Drill 2 – diagonal running

- Use the outside of one foot.
- Use sideways control rather than a direct run.

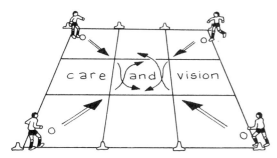

Fig. 5   Drill 2 – diagonal running

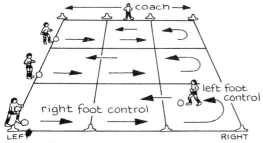

Fig. 6   Drill 3 – sideways movement

Drill 3 – sideways movement

- Look ahead and use both the left and the right foot for control, depending on the movement.

Drill 4 – random movement

This drill can be:

1 totally under the control of the players, or
2 partially controlled by the coach, who commands a change of movement on demand (i.e. with a shout or a whistle).

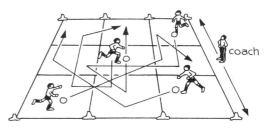

Fig. 7   Drill 4 – random movement

Drill 5 – running against imaginary opponents

This practice has free movement in the area with some obstacles (preferably cones).

- Take the ball up to and away from an imaginary opponent.

Fig. 8   Drill 4 – running against imaginary opponents

Drill 6 – running against conditioned, static opposition

- As with the previous drill, but your opponents are allowed one step towards any ball carrier. (Thus they are, in fact, partially active.)

The maximum number of ball carriers for this

Fig. 9 Drill 6 – running against conditioned, static opposition

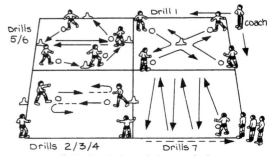

Fig. 11 Individual techniques being taught in group practices

practice is 12–15, while the maximum number of opposition players is 6–9.

Drill 7 – running against conditioned, moving opposition

The opposition for this practice is confined to certain sectors. There is no tackling to begin with, just 'closing down' work.

■ Aim to travel safely from A to B with the ball.

Fig. 10 Drill 7 – running against conditioned, moving opposition

Coaching advice to the player

1. Experiment within the demands of each practice.
2. If you are inactive during a practice, then *watch* and *imitate* those players who you think are doing well.

Advice to coaches

1. Organise demonstrations which highlight each drill quickly and simply, then step back and watch the action.
2. Do not stop positive action; if there are problems, take the individual out of the

practice, offer him some advice and then slot him back into the drill quietly.
3. Encourage the players to generate fast, sharp footwork.

Disguise

It is one thing to develop techniques when running with the ball in open space, unchallenged, but quite another to perform those same techniques when faced with an opponent. Quite often the easiest option when confronted by an opposition defender is to get both the ball and your team-mates into space beyond that opponent by executing an accurate, appropriately timed and weighted pass. But to do this is partly to withdraw from the challenge that the defender poses the ball carrier, that is to try and get past him while still in possession. This forces players into what has been called the 'predictability' of the pass. Of course, passing itself can be a difficult task, especially if the player is under pressure and there is no guarantee of success. Nevertheless, few players seem to want to accept the challenge of taking on the defence and so few become good dribblers of the ball, since they lack the confidence to use running speed, ball speed, disguise and feints in their play.

This may be because coaches do not allow sufficient opportunity for the necessary physical and technical qualities to emerge and be developed, or because they do not know enough about how to build disguise and feinting techniques. These techniques are also known as 'tricks', and they enable the dribbler to disturb the stability of the oncoming defender. Tricks can help get a player out of awkward situations or enable him to advance into more vital attacking areas. Given that soccer is a game where players have to work in very restricted areas, always being pressurised and closed down by markers, you would think that every footballer would want to have a few tricks up his sleeve! The following section offers players some techniques and conditioned practices which will enhance their disguise on the ball.

Technical information

1.   Initiate disguise by moving various parts of the body together or in sequence as you meet the defender.
2.   Make as if to kick the ball in one direction, then work over the ball and kick it to a different area of the pitch.
3.   Focus beyond the ball at the opponent's legs and midriff so that you can monitor his responses quickly and react accordingly.
4.   Give false verbal and non-verbal (especially facial) information to the defender.
5.   Entice the defender towards you.
6.   Adopt a good stable base, drop your hips and lean forwards slightly as you attempt the initial disguise going into any dribble.

Coaching advice to the player

- Practise the techniques against an imaginary opponent until there is a certain flow to the dribbling sequence.
- Be confident and remember that mistakes will occur. Aim to dominate your opponent by your actions.

Objective

To encourage the use of disguise and deception while running with the ball.

Drill 1 – typical body feint using the whole body

- Stay relaxed and upright on the ball as you see a defender just beginning to come towards you.
- Lean forwards and step over the ball towards the opponent's defensive space as if you are about to attack, then check out/back.
- Watch where the opponent goes!
- Repeat this disguise more than once before

initiating an actual dribbling or passing movement.

Drill 2 – typical body feint using fast leg movement

- Run with the ball in a balanced position, keeping the ball situated in front of you so that you can move in either direction using either foot.
- Lean towards one direction with the upper body, then quickly follow this with a fast step-over action to take you across the ball; hopefully the defender will respond to this.
- Drive back off the step-over foot and then move away with the ball using the outside of the other foot.

Drill 3 – typical ball feint with fast movement of the feet and a dummy pass

- Run and meet a pass delivered from the side.
- Make as if you are about to pass the ball immediately, continuing the directional flow of the ball and using a full backswing as if you were striking the ball.
- Instead of hitting the ball, step over it, go beyond and across it and drive it away in the other direction.

Drill 4 – typical passing feint

- Receive a pass and control the ball.
- Step back from the ball momentarily and 'look' to pass, even gesticulating to the player to whom you are intending to pass.
- Move into the intended pass, then check and drag the ball across in front of you and drive away quickly with the ball on the outside of your opposite foot.

Drill 5 – body and ball feint 1 (no opposition)

- Work in a grid with 4 players.
- Experiment with body and ball feints against a static object.

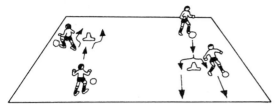

Fig. 12 Drill 5 – body and ball feint 1 (no opposition)

Drill 6 – body and ball feint 2 (with opposition)

- Attack the defender head-on.
- Work in groups of 5 in a grid, dribbling from each end.

The defenders' activity is limited, that is they are not allowed to tackle.

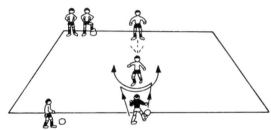

Fig. 13 Drill 6 – body and ball feint 2 (with opposition)

Drill 7 – body and ball feint 3

As with previous drill but slightly more intense.

- The defender is allowed one challenge.
- You can either travel through the grid (ABC) or trick the defender with a quick turn in zone B (ABA).

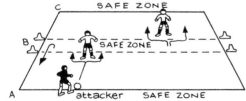

Fig. 14 Drill 7 – body and ball feint 3

Drill 8 – 'Options'

You have a number of potential passing options in this drill, and you can use these once or not at all.

Fig. 15 Drill 8 – 'options'

- Try to make the defender think you are going to pass when in fact this is the last resort.
- Occasionally pass so that you keep the defender guessing.

Drill 9

- Aim to throw the defender off balance so that you can travel beyond the mid-line and into the square.

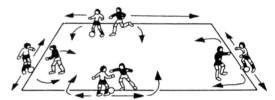

Fig. 16 Drill 9

Drill 10 – passing feints on receiving the ball (1)

- Get a feeder to pass or roll a ball in to your feet.
- Dummy pass on receiving the ball, work over the ball and move away in a different direction.
- Pass the ball back to the feeder and repeat the exercise.

Fig. 17 Drill 10 – passing feints on receiving the ball (1)

Drill 11 – passing feints on receiving the ball (2)

- Make as if to pass forwards to the left.
- Check at the last moment and drag the ball behind your body.
- Return the ball to the feeder.

This drill can also be performed by taking the ball across in front of you.

drag back.

pretended pass direction

Fig. 18   Drill 11 – passing feints on receiving the ball (2)

To conclude this section on running with the ball and deception on the ball, it is worth noting that the ball carrier is the most vital player on the field at any single time. All of the other players take their cue from him, particularly the nearest defender and most obvious recipient of the ball, and they will all be watching the ball carrier's movements, looking for a key as to what they should do next. Thus if you can make the defender misinterpret your visual and verbal cues, you and your team are at an advantage. The single danger is, I suppose, that you may be such a virtuoso player that even your own team-mates cannot read your game, and therefore they will never be able to work properly off your skills. You need, therefore, to blend individuality and team cohesion, unpredictability and predictability.

STRIKING THE BALL: BASIC TECHNIQUES

Once you are feeling comfortable on the ball, you can begin to place yourself in situations where you have to strike the ball in a variety of ways in order to transfer it with accuracy to another team-mate. Indeed, one or two of the practices which centre on disguise using a potential receiver (see previous chapter) require basic passing skills. The time spent on building up confidence in working with the ball and maintaining balance and composure, will seem well worth while when it comes to learning striking or kicking skills. It is essential, for example, in the earlier dribbling and deception practices, to experiment using both feet so that when you come to striking the ball in the game situation you will not be limited by your passing and shooting ability. Also, this will ensure that you do not develop a one-sidedness which can sometimes lead to a complete reliance on one foot for the execution of the basic skills. In the modern game, at whatever level, a player who can use both feet has the opportunity to become a more complete, and therefore

potentially more dangerous, footballer. At the élite level, professional football is played at great speed, and so time to dwell on the ball is limited and space to operate in gets quickly closed down. Thus to be able to play well on both feet is not so much a luxury as an essential commodity for play.

When striking a soccer ball the main thing to look for initially is a high level of accuracy resulting from any ball contact. So the larger the surface that makes contact with the ball, the better. For passing this means that the main techniques are contact with the inside of the foot, and instep (top of the foot) contact. Variations on the pass are essential in soccer in order to lift and curve the ball over and around the opponent. Thus techniques using outside or inside of the instep contact are also vital.

An understanding of the basic mechanics of striking is helpful when it comes to applying the various techniques to the game situation. Players often try to make specific types of pass in certain areas of the pitch. For example, a traditional winger or a midfield player breaking wide ought to be able to strike a pass, applying spin or rotary motion applied to the ball at impact, which curves across and behind a defender while at the same time moving away from the goalkeeper. A team which has a large number of players capable of applying these deft touches will have a great many creative options.

The following section will examine these striking techniques, highlighting important technical information. In addition, different forms of ball contact will be placed in a context, so that a number of skills practices and conditioned situations will be available to players of various abilities.

General principles

1. Maintain a *stable base* while striking.
2. Keep the *head completely steady* (eyes on the ball) before, during and after contact.
3. Develop a *positive rhythm* in striking, aiming for an *optimal timing* on contact.

The mechanics of striking

The two mechanical points which follow need to be understood, since they relate to the fact that in striking the ball several muscle groups linked around a number of joints are being brought into action.

1. Develop a *full range of movement*, to enable all the muscle groups and joints to be used to maximum effect.
2. First initiate movement in the large muscle groups, then progressively bring in smaller muscle groups. This will facilitate a *sequence for striking*, allowing an optimal ordering to any technique.

These two latter points demonstrate that there are set phases to any passing or striking action, much like in any sport when performing what may be called a 'closed' skill (i.e. where the performer focuses totally on the physical activity and does not have to worry about other variables such as an approaching defender). Footballers do have some moments in a game when they can concentrate totally on the mechanics of the skill, for example when striking the ball at set-pieces. If we look at any soccer kick we can identify a number of recognisable and distinct phases and these are shown in the following table.

	Phase	Player action
1	initial preparation	striding into the ball
2	loading movement	striking leg is taken back
3	down swing	leg is brought down through the ball
4	contact	striking moment
5	follow-through	striking leg swings through, plus upper body forwards movement

Given that striking the ball from set-pieces is so important, it is worth rehearsing the action in your mind, visualising each of the various stages. This psychological preparation will help you on the day.

Inside of the foot technique

This is the most common method of kicking and passing the ball. It allows for maximum safety and accuracy in its execution. The only drawback is the fact that once a player is into the down swing with his striking leg, he is committed to that type of pass. Other types of pass also allow for a last-second 'check out' and the possible use of deception. The inside of the foot technique is easily read by a good defender, who can then anticipate the direction. However, it is the basic striking method for close passing inter-plays and for low and volleyed passes in particular.

Technical information

1. Place the non-striking foot alongside the ball, with the foot pointing in line with the direction of the strike.
2. The hip of the kicking leg rotates on the down swing after a limited backswing. This strike often requires accuracy rather than power, hence there is a limited backswing.
3. When you make contact with the ball, lean forwards slightly with the upper body.
4. The follow-through is a limiting one, and is linear.

Inside of the foot technique. This basic short passing technique ensures maximum accuracy

Instep kick technique

This is the most natural striking method for most players, especially when they are seeking to impart great power, for example with shots at goal, long passes and clearances. For this technique the player takes the striking leg through a full range of movement. Because of the nature of the contact with the ball, it is a strike that requires great co-ordination, and considerable practice is necessary in order to master this technique. Those players who manage to do so are the most lethal of dead-ball strikers at set-pieces.

The contact point of the instep kick technique

Technical information

1. Place the non-striking foot alongside the ball, with the foot pointing in line with the direction of strike. The supporting leg is slightly bent at the knee, allowing for a drive up and through as contact is made.
2. Use a full backswing for power on the kicking leg, and a limited backswing for crisper, short passes or possible movement into a feint to shoot or pass.
3. The instep makes full contact with the ball, and the ankle is fixed at full extension.
4. The follow-through is completed with the body-weight being 'thrown' behind the ball as power is required.

Outside of the foot technique

Many footballers strike the ball with the outside of the foot as this gives them some variety of pass, depending on how hard the ball is struck and the way the striking foot works through the ball. This type of strike is often used for simple, fast-tempo first time passes, and also for long passes or set-piece strikes when there is a need to curve the ball. The latter is particularly useful because the defenders gain no immediate visual information as to where the ball might go, unless they spot a 'toeing in' of the striking foot or a pronounced body lean. The curved ball is a favourite ploy used by many South American players, notably the Brazilians and Argentinians, and the rarefied air of these countries further exaggerates the 'bend' in the flight of the ball.

Outside of the foot technique at contact point

Technical information

1. The striking foot is placed alongside the ball, while the foot points in line with the direction of the strike.
2. The kicking leg moves through either a controlled backswing or a full backswing, depending on whether power or disguise is needed.
3. At the point of contact the angle of the foot in relation to the placement of the ball is rotated slightly inwards and full extended.
4. The follow-through is performed with full leg extension.

A crisper, quicker execution is generated than in the instep kick.

Instep technique for the curved pass

Inside of the instep kicking technique

This type of kick has similar properties to the previous strike in that one possible result is a curved flight path of the ball. It is often used when the player needs to chip a ball into space because he cannot perform a direct ground pass. Also, it tends to be the traditional strike when targeting attacking players for any aerial assault on the opposition's goal, and when aiming long balls from defence to forward players on an attacking run.

Technical information

1. The striking foot is placed in line with the ball, but a more pronounced gap is evident between the ball and the supporting leg. This supporting leg has the more obvious bend as the body needs to work under, up and through the ball in order to create lift.
2. The upper body shows a clear lateral lean over the supporting leg.
3. The kicking leg moves through a controlled backswing, coming in a direction across the ball because of the body's position and the angle of the approach run (which is about 30–40°).
4. At the point of contact the ankle is extended and held firm, while the toes point downwards and slightly outwards.
5. The follow-through involves full leg extension with the body-weight being held back rather than transferred into the strike.

Follow-through for the curved pass with full leg extension

Passing in a game situation

It is generally very easy to develop technical competence in passing in the relative isolation of the coaching grid. But at some stage these techniques have to be developed sufficiently to cope with the attacking, containing and defensive strategies of actual play.

Certain components need to be present in

any pass or strike if it is to have a measure of success. Thus the pass has to be:

1   well timed
2   accurate
3   correctly weighted (degree of power at execution)
4   disguised.

Timing

Timing involves effectively sequencing the action of any strike from the preparation phase right through to the completion of the follow-through. It also is linked to the player's ability to know how to read a situation and to his skill at performing a timely release of the ball. Clearly, the need for sound peripheral vision is paramount here and this is a key variable which affects release.

Accuracy

Coupled with timing of release is accuracy. Accuracy is dictated by the player's positioning in relation to the ball and the type of ball contact. As has been said, the side of the foot pass is the most accurate, for it creates the biggest and most controlled contact with the ball. It also allows for a clear linear passage of the striking foot as it works through the ball immediately prior to and after contact.

Weighting

This is the component that invariably fails all players at some stage. In a game situation the passing player's target is often on the move or is in a space which can be closed off if the weighting is too light. Footballers need to consider the speed of movement of their intended target, and must hit the ball with sufficient power so that as the receiver gets the ball it poses him little or no control problems.

Of course all of these factors must come together in the execution of a pass. At the élite level the game is played at such a pace that 'forward thinking' is vital, and has to be superimposed on high levels of technical efficiency. Furthermore, forward thinking is a component which is both psychologically and temporally (time) determined. Ball transference, and with it ball speed, are invariably very quick in élite football, so clearly excellence should be regarded as a pre-requisite in order that the

player can concentrate on these other factors of play. At other levels, where the pressure from defenders is not so acute, players should be encouraged to select the correct passing options and to develop technical mastery in the game environment. The following is a series of individual technique drills and conditioned group practices which will help mould the essential passing and striking skills of any outfield player.

Striking and passing practices

Objectives

1.   To develop individual technical competence in all the essential kicking techniques.
2.   To relate these techniques to the game situation and build a strategical competence with respect to passing and striking opportunities.
3.   To introduce players to reception techniques which can be built on at the same time in the conditioned small-sided games.

Individual practices

1.   Kick a static ball against a wall (sectioned off as for target practice). Use a side of the foot kick.
2.   Kick a ball towards a wall after throwing and dropping it directly in front of you. Variety can be achieved by:

■   striking the ball on the volley, or half-volley
■   throwing the ball up to the left and the right so as to generate a hip-turn kick.

3.   Kicking a ball repeatedly against a wall using all the different types of kick. Variety can be achieved by:

■   conditioning the options (i.e. all side of the foot volleys where the ball is kept up off the ground)
■   developing a routine, carrying out particular techniques in rotation.

4.   Ball juggling, i.e. keeping a ball aloft using both feet and all types of contact with the foot.

Group practices

Drill 1 – striking and passing practice (1)

Work in pairs with one partner as a controlled feeder (A).

- A rolls the ball underarm to (i) the feet and (ii) either side of player B.
- A throws the ball to (i) the feet and (ii) either side of player B.

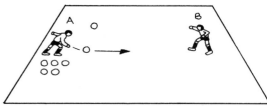

Fig. 19   Drill 1 – striking and passing practice (1)

Drill 2 – striking and passing practice (2)

Work in pairs as in the previous practice. In this exercise, however, power and accuracy come into play as the striker is asked to hit the target.

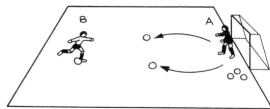

Fig. 20   Drill 2 – striking and passing practice (2)

Drill 3 – striking for accuracy

The feeder (B) rolls the ball back gently (or places the ball) for striker A who executes:

- a side of the foot short strike
- a side of the foot lifted strike
- an inside of the instep strike.

Players C and D act as retrievers.

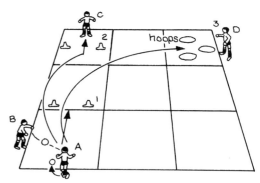

Fig. 21   Drill 3 – striking for accuracy

Drill 4 – pressure passing routine

Players move into practice quickly. The player in the middle plays each alternate high and ground ball back to a feeder, turning to face each feeder in succession.

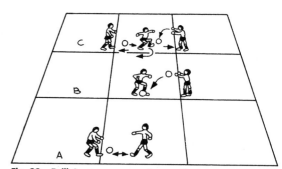

Fig. 22   Drill 4 – pressure passing routine

BALL RECEPTION AND CONTROL

Basic techniques

The previous drills and practices with partners involved the simple striking of the ball by one active player. When we move on to situations where all players are active, advice on the techniques and skills involved in receiving a ball becomes necessary. Only then can we enter into partner and group practices centred around passing and control of the ball.

At this stage we will only be dealing with technical points relating to the skill of receiving balls passed to the feet. Advanced types of reception will be dealt with later in this chapter in combination with the skills of shielding the ball and turning in order to attack a defender.

Controlling the ball with the inside of the foot

Technical information

1. Adopt the ready position (i.e. where the body-weight is well distributed over a firm base) so that you can move forwards, backwards and laterally towards any pass.
2. Watch the ball all the way until contact is made. This is vital if you are to gain maximum information about the power and flight of the ball and decide what angle is necessary to receive the ball on the foot.
3. Once you have received it get into the direct line of the ball.
4. Control the ball so that there is little or no rebound off the foot. You can do this by trapping the ball with the inside of the foot and applying downward force.
5. The weight of the incoming pass can also be absorbed by pulling back with the controlling foot immediately on receiving of the ball. By being relaxed and responsive the ball speed can be dissipated by a quick recoil of the lower leg. This effectively kills the ball speed and allows the ball to stay conveniently at your feet.

Coaching advice to the player

1. Total concentration is required for effective ball reception skills, irrespective of their simplicity or sophistication.
2. Exaggerate the mechanics of the skill so as to 'groove' the method.
3. Always remain relaxed and ready to receive any ball whether the play is close at hand or some distance away.

Striking, passing, receiving and controlling the ball are essential techniques which need repeated practice if they are to become automatic and intuitive. Clearly, providing a whole range of practice 'lay-outs' is vital here, since these are similar to the patterns the players can expect to find in any match. Imaginative coaches should think about the drills they expose their players to and always seek to offer them something new and stimulating, ranging from highly structured, regimented drills to free, open-ended practice situations. The practices already described are tightly structured and allow for progression. They have been made 'game-like' wherever possible. However, to be truly interactive one extra component has to be added – the defender. Only then do we have in our small-sided practices a microcosm of a game. Also, it is only when we include a defender that we can begin to monitor the progress of our attacking techniques in a true pressure situation.

Passing and basic ball reception practices

Drill 1

For this practice, players work in groups of 4. 1 player controls the ball and then aims for accuracy in passing the ball to his partner at the other end of the grid. The group starts with only 1 ball in play, then advances to 2 balls, only releasing the ball when the target player is free.

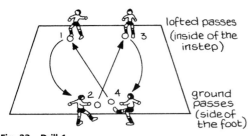

Fig. 23   Drill 1

Drill 2

For this practice, players work in groups of 5. 1 player controls the ball and then passes it to a specified player. The passer sprints to the target

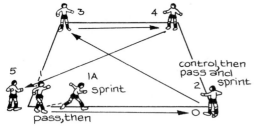

Fig. 24   Drill 2

20

player's position after passing. The group starts with ground passes, then moves on to aerial passes and a mixture of both.

Drill 3

The players work as a large unit with 2 or 3 balls. 2 players sprint for 30 seconds from one end of the corridor to the other, then another two runners replace them. The players who are passing the balls have to concentrate on the runners passing down the corridor and also watch for the balls being crossed.

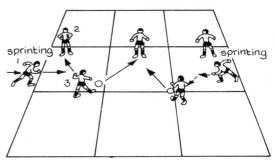

Fig. 25   Drill 3

Drill 4

This practice has 4 players working in a grid. Here the emphasis is on accurate passing with 2 pairs of players and 4 balls in play. The players must take care to synchronise their passing so that no player is faced with receiving 2 balls at once. The secret is to call and look before passing.

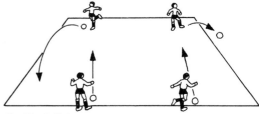

Fig. 26   Drill 4

Drill 5

The players work in groups of 12 split into 4 groups of 3, with 4 balls in play. Each player must dribble the ball to the middle and then pass to the right before running straight across the grid.

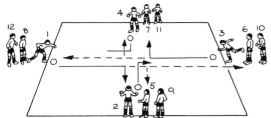

routine 2 (4 balls) players 1,2,3,4 dribble and pass to the right, then run across ....then the whole cycle keeps going.

Fig. 27 Drill 5

Drill 6

This practice has three types of progression.

1. *Zone 1.* Players 1 and 3 and players 2 and 4 hit aerial balls back and forth to each other.
2. *Zone 2.* Players 1 and 3 and players 2 and 4 hit alternate aerial and ground passes, moving sideways after hitting the ball to receive the returned pass.
3. *Zone 3.* Players 1 and 3 and players 2 and 4 hit controlled aerial passes continuously. There are 4 balls in play in this zone.

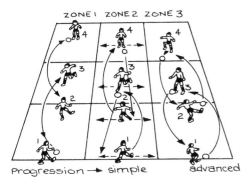

Fig. 28 Drill 6

Drill 7

Working in groups of 3, the players hit close volleys continuously with the side of the foot.

Fig. 29 Drill 7

The middle player turns to receive volleys from the players on the outside. The players on the outside lift the ball over the middle player. Players should not be too far apart. The practice starts with an underarm throw to the middle player.

Advanced ball reception techniques

Each player needs to possess a range of techniques which will allow him to receive and control a variety of passes. In this respect time and space at the vital moment of reception are key factors for concern, since a great deal of pressure is placed upon the player to put his possession of the ball to good use, and to do that he will need to create space for himself. It has to be realised that first-time, lay-off passes are rare in soccer today because of the close marking of all players. Similarly, free passing options are increasingly limited, so players need to become comfortable on the ball and confident that they can shield it and manipulate the primary defender in order to create space. The initial ball control and body movement are fundamental to the development of advanced ball reception techniques. When these techniques are mastered the player will have the

Outside of the foot control. This is often used as the primary control in close passing situations

confidence born of the knowledge that he can dominate the ball. Players need to realise that balls will come to them at various angles and lines of flight and that therefore they need to select quickly and carefully the correct body part to control the ball, bearing in mind variables like their position on the field and the nearest supporting and defensive players.

Technical information

The ball can be controlled by various parts of the body, including the foot (i.e. the instep, the sole, and the inside and outside of the foot), the thigh and the chest. The flight path, line (or direction) and speed of the ball into the player often dictate which part of the body is used and this information needs to be assimilated as quickly as possible by the receiving player. Obviously, if a player is running into space to receive a 40-metre (44-yard) pass, he will have more time to process this information than a player who is tightly marked and about to receive a 5-metre (5-yard) pass. But whatever the circumstances, the first control will be crucial. At the point of contact the player must ensure that the incoming force is taken off the ball so that there is little or no sharp rebound away from his body. Ideally, the ball needs to drop down or stay within about a metre of his feet, because invariably he will need a second attempt at control.

The part of the body used to control the ball

Chest control. The weight is taken off the ball leaving the possibility of deflecting or passing the ball to a team-mate

The upper body is used to direct the ball to the feet of the player for total control

should preferably be large, flat and able to take the weight off the ball through movement. This is most readily achieved with controls using the foot or thigh, but is not always possible with chest controls. Consequently some types of chest control simply divert the incoming ball into space in order to create time for the receiver or an attacking opportunity for another team-mate. The thigh is a particularly good surface both because it can be retracted quickly and because it consists of a large muscle group

Thigh control making good use of a large cushioning area

with a natural 'give', allowing fine control. A whole body area can be offered up to the ball on its own, as with a thigh or chest control, while on other occasions the ball may be trapped between the body surface and the ground, as with the use of the foot or lower leg. The controlling surfaces of the foot and lower leg are rather small and angular, but this weakness is compensated for by the fact that they are extremities which can be moved rapidly and operated using the ground as a natural control mechanism.

To co-ordinate the control the player needs to create time and space for himself by:

■ positioning himself within the flight path of the ball at a suitable angle for reception
■ adopting a position of readiness early on and selecting an appropriate control surface to receive the ball
■ controlling the ball effectively, depending upon his situation.

Coaching advice to the player

1. Watch the ball all the way.
2. Make an early judgement as to the correct type of control.
3. Move early into line with the incoming ball.
4. Be well balanced at all times.
5. Be aware of the events going on around you.

Of course it is not always possible to control an incoming ball and immediately lay it off to a team-mate. Players should experiment with receiving a pass and moving away from a defender into space. This is most effective if the actions of controlling the ball and moving away can be contained and made to occur simultaneously. The skill is very intricate and requires a great deal of practice, but it is very useful when faced with close marking in game situations. The practices explained later show how this skill can be built both with and without opposition. However, coaches should be aware that progress to situations with opposition should only be considered when all the players involved have exhibited a high level of technical efficiency. Even then, the coach should control the amount of active defence, slowly grading the practices so that full opposition only comes after a period of time.

When defenders or opposition players are brought into practice situations the attacking players need to be made aware of the importance of being able to shield or screen the ball. Quite literally this allows the attacker to partially hide the ball from his opponent by placing his body between the opponent and the ball. Thus the attacker can still play the ball while using his body as an obstacle. Furthermore, he can prevent the primary defender from obtaining a clear route to the ball, thereby making it likely that the defender will commit a foul by 'playing' the attacker and not the ball. Of course, in reality several defenders may home in on the ball carrier, thus making the ability to shield the ball a prized technique.

All the creative skills of the attacking footballer need to come together when faced with an on-the-ball situation. In addition, good decision-making skills and superb fitness are necessary if he is continually to pose problems for his opponents. Attackers have a great deal to do in those moments before they receive a pass. It is often not good enough just to wait for the ball to arrive at your feet. In close marking situations feints and false runs (that is where a player 'suggests' a possible angled run then doubles back on himself) are excellent ways of creating extra space to work in. Also, they enhance a player's repertoire, giving him the initiative and leaving the defender physically and mentally intimidated.

Control practices (unopposed)

Drill 1

The players work in pairs.

The receiver is fed a variety of balls by hand (or foot) along the ground. This forces him to move in all directions in order to control the ball. The basic sequence for the receiver is: look; decide; control; pass. Variety can be introduced if the player uses both feet or a range of foot surface controls.

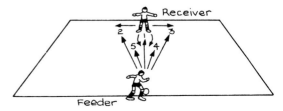

Fig. 30 Drill 1

Drill 2

The players work in pairs as before except that this time the feeder varies the height and angle of balls. The balls should drop within 1–3 ft of the feet.

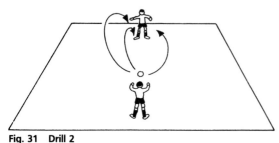

Fig. 31   Drill 2

Drill 3

The players work in groups of 4, passing high balls which are angled across a large area. The passes are varied by aiming (a) at the player, (b) in front of the player and (c) across the player. There are 2 balls in play and these are hit simultaneously.

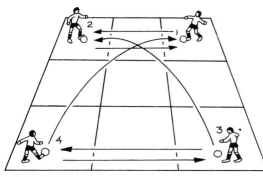

Fig. 32   Drill 3

Drill 4

The players work in groups of 4, split into pairs. Each pair has one player hitting a long pass

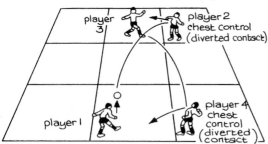

Fig. 33   Drill 4

and his partner deflecting the ball with his chest. The roles are reversed after a set time.

Drill 5

The players work in groups of 4.
   The receivers either hit the ball with the outside of the foot, moving away as soon as it is struck, or hit the ball with the inside of the foot, moving across with the ball under control.

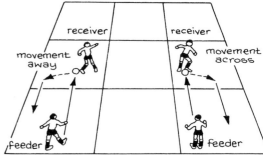

Fig. 34   Drill 5

Control practices (opposed)

Drill 1

The players work in groups of 3.
   A ball is fed in to an attacker who has a start of 5 metres maximum on a defender. The ball is brought under control, the defender approaches the attacker and then the attacker lays the ball back to the feeder. This process is repeated and the players change roles. The defender can become more involved if the attacker moves progressively closer to him (i.e. up to 1metre away).
   The first control should be performed with the foot that is further away from the defender so as to screen the ball.

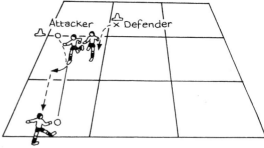

Fig. 35   Drill 1

Drill 2

The players work as a group in pairs. There is 1 nominated defender and 1 nominated attacker. The attacker aims to shield and keep control of the ball as well as 'losing' the defender. The defender is only allowed to close down the attacker; he cannot tackle.

The drill can be varied by asking the defenders, on a command, to close down on a different player. Also, cones may be placed in the grids to act as targets for the attackers to move towards and touch while still controlling the ball.

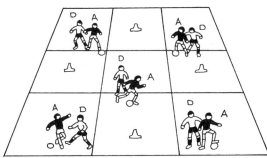

Fig. 36   Drill 2

Drill 3

The players work in groups of 4.
Attacker A moves along a start line and,

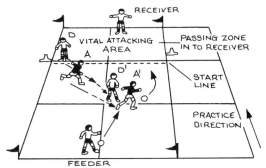

Fig. 37   Drill 3

when he chooses, initiates an angled run back and across a feeder, leaving his defender (D). The receiving player has 2 options. He can:

- pass back to the feeder, turn and sprint behind the defender who is expecting the return pass, or
- turn, face the defender and dribble or push pass beyond him, chasing the ball.

Drill 4

The players work in groups of 3 or 4.
After receiving the ball the attacker uses body feints to make the defender go in the wrong direction. When he has sufficient space the attacker aims to pass to hit a variety of targets. The angle of balls played into the receiver may be varied. Initially, the defender just closes down space but at a later stage he may tackle.

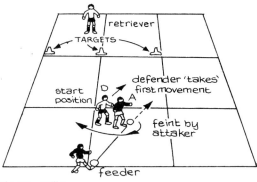

Fig. 38   Drill 4

Drill 5

The players work in groups of 3.
Two players compete for the ball and whoever wins turns and aims to run beyond his opponent either to the safe zone or to the free shooting zone. Competing and winning the ball can be a drill in itself with the emphasis on making a fair, physical challenge.

DEFENDING

Soccer is a game where teams battle to gain possession of the ball. Once they have secured possession they aim to score, and to do this they have to seek a territorial advantage and make sure that their attacking manoeuvres in the opposition's half are productive. This is where defensive techniques and skills come into play. Positive defence is concerned with closing opponents down, denying them the space and the time to build attacking ploys. Good defence is also about pressurising an opponent so that he is not allowed the freedom to be creative and to attack. Defence is the antithesis of the skills involved in running with and dribbling the ball because, from a superficial analysis, it only seems to be concerned with the negation of skill and flair. But this is to view soccer from a biased perspective. While it is true that the game itself and the fans place a higher value on the attacking aspect of play, and the ultimate accolades always go to those players who score the goals, it is important not to denigrate defensive skills. The notion of 'active defence' enables us to see that every player, irrespective of playing position, becomes a defender when his team loses possession. A gifted attacking side is nothing without the ball, and they will still be limited even when they have the ball if they are denied the time and the space in which to operate. Positive defence, with its ultimate objective of winning the ball and keeping it, is the springboard for creating attacking opportunities.

The essential techniques, skills and personal qualities that the defender must possess are as follows.

1.   The ability to *pressurise* attackers by jockeying and containing them.
2.   The ability to *mark* opponents and *channel* them into less attacking positions.
3.   The ability to *tackle* opponents effectively and *dispossess* them.

Tackling comes last in this list because it should be the last resort for the defender when he is being confronted with an attacker in full flight. Indeed, the best defenders are those who seem never to tackle. These players have sufficient physical and psychological presence to expose any error of control by the attacker, enabling them to exit with the ball.

Thus great defenders must possess high levels of:

■ physical strength and size
■ courage and determination
■ discipline
■ confidence and concentration.

Of course, other, more personal, qualities play their part, and there is no such thing as a stereotypical defender.

In the following section the technical qualities of the defender are examined in more detail, and practices are outlined which are specifically designed to develop a player's defensive skills.

Marking techniques

In order to be able to follow an opponent and mark him out of a game a defender has to be well positioned and balanced. Given the great speed of ball there is in passing at the élite level it is clear that a good defence must be based on *close* marking. If passes are controlled and laid off almost instantaneously, then there is little point in being more than a couple of quick strides away from the attacker. A defender will not be able to challenge for the ball or stop an attacker from taking the ball and running at him if he allows the attacker time and space to work in.

Furthermore, any creative or disruptive attacker will aim to get the ball beyond the defender or, better still, take both himself and the ball past the defender. To do this the attacker needs room and potential passing angles, and he also needs the defender to commit himself ineffectively. He achieves this though disguise and deception in his passing and dribbling.

Technical information

1.   Get into a balanced position and keep the feet well spread to facilitate a wide base. Stand

slightly sideways-on with one hip leading, depending on which way the attacker is being channelled, so that it is easy to shift your body-weight rapidly.

2. Focus in on the ball's movements and not those of the attacker's hips and legs.

3. Stay on your feet and do not commit yourself in the initial stages of marking unless you are forced to make a tackle.

Coaching advice to the player

1. Always *remain alert* even though play may not be directly nearby; defence can turn into attack after just one or two quick, penetrative passes, so *concentrate* all the time.

2. When possession is lost *pick up an opposition player quickly*, i.e. perform some 'active' defence immediately.

3. If you are nearest the ball or the opposition ball carrier, close him down and *deny him space*. This may mean going across field or retiring and *making a recovery run* to get to the ball, as well as moving goal-side of your opponent. Again, make up this distance between yourself and the ball carrier *at speed*.

4. When you have closed in on the ball carrier try not to let him turn to face you. Instead use positive marking to *force him backwards or out towards the touch-line* where his movement and pass options automatically diminish. The moment an opponent can turn and face you he has an advantage, because he then has a number of damaging passing options available to him, for example passing behind you. He can also run at you, attempting to beat you with speed or deception, or he can do both.

5. *Try to dictate* what the ball carrier does. Make him do what you want him to do by being the boss both physically and psychologically. Simply denying him space will give you the first 'victory', and you can then continue to chart your dominance over him to encourge positive thought and action.

6. *If you have to commit yourself* to a challenge, *pick your moment carefully*. This is often when the attacker is attempting to turn on to you, because he has to place himself behind the ball, therefore leaving it open to you. In other words, his body no longer hides the ball or prevents you from attempting to win back possession by means of a tackle. This moment often is a fleeting one, so always be well prepared and balanced, and resist any

desire to dive in recklessly if you are not totally ready.

7. Keep talking to your fellow defenders, giving them support and advice as to what is going on around them.

Objective

To give the defensive player an awarenes of those factors which contribute to sound marking, i.e. active defence, close proximity and continual pressure.

Marking practices

Drill 1

The players work in groups of 4 with a defender, a receiver, a feeder and an attacker.

The defender attempts to close down the attacker and force him back so that he cannot pass forwards to the receiver. The defender stands at the side and only moves when the ball is passed into the grid. He is successful if the attacker is forced to pass the ball or runs out of space.

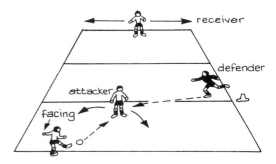

Fig. 39 Drill 1

Drill 2

In this practice the defender closes in on the attacker by making an angled run and limiting the attacker's opportunity to pass to the receiver. The receiver is allowed a range of movement within a set area and the defender must chaperone the attacker down a channel towards the touch-line which is furthest away from the receiver.

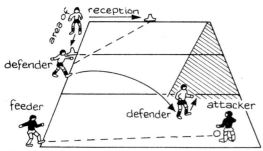

Fig. 40 Drill 2

Drill 3

The players work in pairs.

The defender has to make a quick, angled recovery run to drop in ahead of the attacker who shoots at the small goal once he gets into the last (shaded) section of the grid. The defender should attempt to push the attacker as wide as possible away from the goal, so that any shooting angle will be extremely oblique.

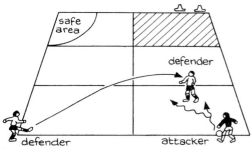

Fig. 41 Drill 3

Drill 4

The players work in groups of 4.

The defender attempts to force the attacker down one of the touch-lines, that is down a narrowing corridor which is away from the goal. When one attacker is thwarted another sets off

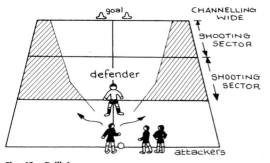

Fig. 42 Drill 4

and the defender has to repeat the exercise. The attacker must choose one particular flank to start his attack.

Inevitably, these drills will place the defender in situations where he has to develop his ability to close down attackers, pressurise them into making mistakes, or force them into 'safe' areas away from goal. They will also expose his tackling ability. When he feels he is really being threatened and is committed to a challenge, he will have to execute a firm tackle. He may also be given an opportunity to tackle if the attacker makes a mistake and leaves the ball momentarily available to be contested.

There are a number of tackles that a defender must be proficient in performing, notably:

- the front block tackle
- the side block tackle
- the ground block tackle
- the sliding tackle.

The following section looks at the techniques involved in each of these tackle situations.

Tackling techniques

Few soccer coaching experts concentrate on the virtues of defence and the fundamental necessity for all players to have sound techniques in this less glamorous aspect of the game. Players and coaches should look at games, playing techniques and skills as a totality. The modern game extols the value of having defenders with great skill at moving forwards and initiating attacks. It also should place on a pedestal those strikers who become aggressive and abrasive defenders the second the ball is lost in attack. There is a great danger of placing skills and essential techniques into compartments which are too narrow. The more complete the individual's skills, the better the team will be as a whole. If strikers can perform a vital function by chasing and tackling opponents, *and* defenders can move forwards and attack, then we have the beginnings of an excellent team, technically.

The following tackling techniques and practices require strength, commitment, concentration and precision in their execution.

The front block tackle

This tackle is made when the defender confronts an attacking player head-on, with his body square-on to the ball. Often, these tackles are performed by midfield players when the ball runs free in the middle third of the pitch and two players are in direct competition for possession.

Both players exhibit sound technique for the front block tackle in this head-on confrontation

Here one player enters the contact point poorly balanced

Technical information

1. The player makes contact with the ball with the side of his foot, often at the same time as his opponent.
2. The player must enter this contact situation (with the ball and the opposing player) at force.
3. A sound base is required, with the weight being placed over and through the ball. Hence it is vital to have the supporting foot in close to the ball at contact.
4. The whole body should be working through the ball, tensed and active. Upper-body lean into the tackle is essential.
5. If the whole action has been well co-ordinated, maximum force will be applied at the point of the tackle.

Coaching advice to the player

1. Keep your eye on the ball.
2. Keep your upper-body weight forward.
3. Accelerate into the tackle.
4. Apply maximum force through the ball at the tackle.

The side block tackle

This tackle is performed either when an attacker has gone partially beyond the defender, or when the defender attempts to close down an attempted angled pass. It is also used as a defensive tackle by fullbacks or wide defenders when attacking players seek to initiate crosses or passes around the back of the defence.

Technical information

1. The tackle is made with an outstretched leg, so balance is vital.
2. Timing when to initiate the tackle is of paramount importance.
3. Assume a stable base so that when the tackle has to be made it can be made quickly.

Coaching advice to players

1. Watch the ball and not the feet or hips of your opponent.
2. Watch out for feints or disguised shots.

The ground block tackle

In this tackle the defender goes to ground as he commits himself. The tackle is made when an attacker is running at or, more probably, across the defender. It is usually executed when an attacker has found some space or when he cannot be closed down by a front block or side block tackle. Thus the defender elects to tackle before the attacker goes beyond him with the ball, and sometimes he will throw himself in early in order to claim the ball.

Technical information

1.   Stay on your feet as long as possible then accelerate into the ball. You can do this by dropping into the tackle and sinking the hips, which will allow you to go to ground quickly.
2.   Partially flex the contact leg and keep it as firm as possible, preferably anchoring it by the heel to the ground behind the ball. Your body-weight should be as far forwards as possible.
3.   Your arms make contact with the ground and support your body-weight as force is applied in the tackle.

Coaching advice to the player

Be patient and only commit yourself to this sort of tackle if it is really essential. The minute you go to ground you risk isolating yourself from play if the tackle is missed.

Ground block tackle. The defender has purposely gone to ground to win the ball

The sliding tackle

This tackle is the defender's last chance once the attacking player has gone beyond him. To perform the tackle the defender has to go to ground and slide into the ball, taking it away from the attacking player with his outside leg. The sliding tackle is the most effective tackle if timed well, but the most disastrous tackle if executed poorly, because it leaves the defender on the ground with no chance of returning to the play in time to halt the progress of the attacker. The tackle can be used most successfully near to the touch-line when the ball can be taken off the foot of the attacker and out of play. It is without doubt the most exhilarating tackle, especially when the defender gets to his feet sharply to begin his own attack with the ball, thereby instantly turning defence into offence.

Technical information

1.   Take a full backswing on the tackling foot and throw it at and beyond the ball.
2.   Attempt to trap the ball wherever possible so that you gain possession from the tackle.
3.   Drop the supporting leg quickly, allow your hips to sink and let your body go into a semi-prone position immediately prior to contact.
4.   At the point of contact you should be on your side with your upper hip rolling in towards the ground as the tackle is made.

The sliding tackle. The attacker has gone beyond the defender and the slide tackle is the last resort

Coaching advice to the player

1. Timing is crucial.
2. Go into and out of the tackle at speed.
3. Ensure that you make a clean contact with the ball and not the player; this is easy to do from behind and side-on.

Objectives

To develop tackling techniques and build critical decision-making skills as to the timing and choice of tackles.

Many of the previous marking drills can be repeated with tackling as an added component within the practice.

Tackling practices

Drill 1

This is an intensive tackling practice for 1 defender taking on a group of attackers individually.

The player has to defend a line and execute a front block tackle where possible; he may resort to other types of tackle if an attacker gets beyond him.

Fig. 43   Drill 1

Drill 2

The players work in groups of 4 with 3 players dribbling/running with a ball and one active defender who attempts to win balls and/or knock them out of the grid.

Fig. 44   Drill 2

Drill 3

The players work in groups of 3.

On a command all 3 players run out and slide tackle, trapping the ball and dribbling it back to the start-line before going back for another ball. This practice emphasises the importance of getting back on to your feet quickly and also executing the 'gather' of the ball carefully.

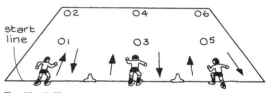

Fig. 45   Drill 3

Drill 4

The players work in groups of 4.

3 players advance slowly down a grid and a defender confronts each of them in turn, performing:

- a front block tackle
- a ground block tackle
- a sliding tackle.

The sequence of tackles has to follow this pattern because after the first tackle the two remaining players will be beyond the defender.

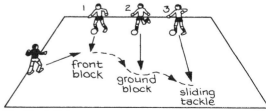

Fig. 46   Drill 4

'Total' soccer strategy

The main aim for a soccer team is to play a 'total' game, with every player contributing to both attack and defence. Thus the goalkeeper is far more than just a saver of goals; he often becomes an attacking player by means of his long kicks, his quick, long throws and his ability to make clearances direct to strikers who act as 'target' men. Likewise, all outfield players are both attackers and defenders, the only variable being whether or not the player is in control of the ball. In defensive terms the most vital role is performed by the primary defender, that is the player who is first to the ball and who attempts to restrict any forward movement to goal. His function, along with any other players who can supply immediate defensive support, is to force the opposition to build-up gradually towards their attack, thereby allowing valuable time for the defence to strategically regroup to cope with the impending pressure. Thus although your team may be on the defensive you can exert your own pressure swiftly and effectively, forcing a turn-over and regaining possession.

Ultimately, of course, sound defence is about exerting such pressure on the opposition that they do not score or even get a chance to shoot at goal. Match analysis statistics show that many goals are scored from 4 passes or less, with successful moves beginning deep in the attacking team's own half. In such instances the function of the primary defender is of the greatest importance, since he has to curb the potentially rapid flow of the opposition's attack by reacting with speed of thought and action. The excuse that 'He wasn't my man' is heard only when players' roles are rigidly demarcated, thus militating against 'team' play. In any match the most effective defence is that which is able to be flexible while retaining the structure of primary defender, secondary defenders (those within 5–10 metres (5.5–11yd) of the primary defender) and the larger 'unit' of defence.

The following drills examine the roles of defenders by means of simple practices for a defence partnership.

Drill 1

This practice has players working in groups of 4 with 1 attacker, 1 feeder and 2 defenders.

The attacker aims to take the ball, under control, from point A to point B. The function of the first defender is to restrict the attacker's ability to turn and delay him. The second defender covers at an appropriate distance and angle and talks to his partner in defence.

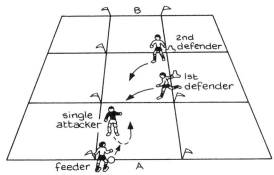

Fig. 47   Drill 1

These drills represent a microcosm of the game's offence/defence structure, because as well as concentrating on what they themselves are doing, the defenders also have to communicate and watch each other's actions. In addition, they have to be close enough together to combat any sudden attack, especially if that attack has got beyond the first defender by virtue of pace or disguise, and they must also be aware of the larger territory they have to protect. Finally, they should consider their role as a defensive 'team', that is to deny the attackers the opportunity to dribble or pass forwards and force them across and out of play.

Marking techniques are even more important when it comes to game situations which are larger than 1 v. 1. Here the supporting players perform a crucial role, helping the primary defender by means of their verbal and non-verbal cues and advice. These players have to remember to stay goal-side of an opponent and also to mark him closely or follow him on whatever runs for the ball or decoys he attempts. These are factors which we will look at in greater detail in the section on off-the-ball skills, since they are especially related to the ability to create and close down space in attack and defence.

SHOOTING

A great deal of the coaching advice given to attacking players concentrates either on teaching them how to get beyond defenders and into space to receive a penetrating pass, or on how to improve their dribbling technique. However, it is also crucial that the attacker is taught to invade the area in and around the opposition's penalty area. Of course, taking on the responsibility of shooting and being a team's main goal-scorer requires considerable mental as well as physical courage. Consequently, those primary attackers whose function it is to score goals have to possess an unswerving confidence in their own ability if they are to reach high levels of consistency in converting into goals the few chances which come their way in a match.

It is a strange paradox that while nearly everything a team attempts to do in moving forwards with the ball is geared towards creating a scoring opportunity, few players are capable of converting that opportunity into a goal. The most obvious way of resolving this dilemma is to get *all* the players to practise the techniques involved in striking the ball within conditioned practices that resemble the match environment. If you have access to a number of easily transportable goals with loose netting you should be able to set up a number of shooting training areas. Also, you could try 'loading' training so that there is a continual emphasis on goal-scoring skills. Finally, through conducting objective game analysis using video and statistics, a player might come to see that his weakness in the vital scoring area is physiological (e.g. lack of speed) of psychological (e.g. slow reaction time).

Although clinical 'finishing' is the hallmark of any great striker, the skill should not be confined to a single player. One of the great strengths of the Brazilian teams over the years has been that nearly every outfield player is a superb striker of the ball and is acutely aware of how best to get to the goal. This takes pressure off the nominated striker and indirectly makes his job easier.

Much of the striker's skill is instinctive and rests on his powers of intuition in and around the goal-mouth. However, if all players are keen to score and have a positive attitude when entering the final third of the pitch, then the psychological burden is shared – as is the praise should the ball go into the net! Thus all players should be encouraged to want to score, and to get into the shooting zone so as to be available to make those all important 'assists'.

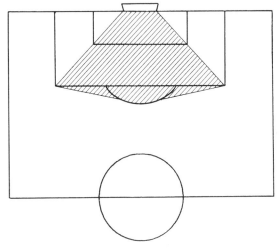

Fig. 48   The primary shooting zone

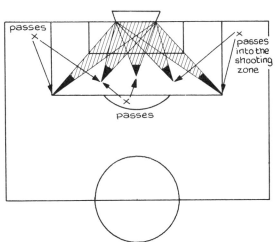

Fig. 49   Some of the possible shooting angles. Note that there is a greater likelihood of success in front of goal as more of the target is on view

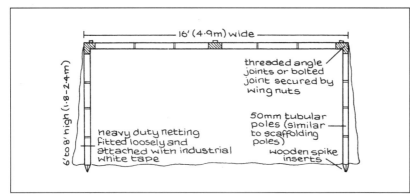

16' (4.9m) wide

6' to 8' high (1.8–2.4m)

threaded angle joints or bolted joint secured by wing nuts

heavy duty netting fitted loosely and attached with industrial white tape

50mm tubular poles (similar to scaffolding poles)

wooden spike inserts

Fig. 50 A home-made portable goal: a valuable and realistic piece of apparatus for shooting practice, approximately $\frac{2}{3}$ full width

Body position at contact point for a shot at goal

The follow-through. Note how the player keeps his head steady

Coaching advice to the player

Advice on shooting should be simple and concise, so that players do not have too much information to ponder. The basic points should be emphasised time and again, with the coach (or another player) monitoring improvements and offering positive feedback.

The main points for primary shooters to remember are as follows.

- Decide to shoot early and minimise any delay (i.e. aim for speed of thought and action).
- Strike with a mixture of power and accuracy.
- Take an early look where possible, and aim to hit the most exposed area of the goal.
- Keep your head steady, with your eyes on the ball.
- Generate reliable preparation, contact and follow-through phases in striking the ball, so as to create a rhythm in your shooting.

Objective

The following practices should help to develop shooting techniques and the skill of finishing in match-like situations.

Shooting practices

Drill 1

The players work in groups of 3.

The first player strikes a stationary ball with the instep of his foot. The second player uses the side of his foot to strike a moving ball which is fed in from the side. The third player receives a ball fed in from the side by hand and volleys it on the turn.

The players all shoot at an undefended goal to begin with, but a goalkeeper may be added at a later stage.

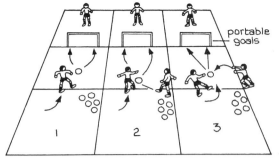

Fig. 51   Drill 1

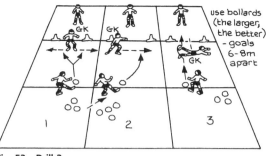

Fig. 53   Drill 3

Drill 2

The players work in groups of 3.

The players strike balls varying in angle, proximity to goal and preparation time. The first player uses the inside of his instep to strike a moving ball which is fed from in front of him. This results in a curved ball. The second player strikes a moving ball fed from behind. He faces the goal and hits an instep drive first time. The third player volleys the ball head-on and on the turn, close in to goal.

As in the previous practice the players shoot initially at an undefended goal, with a goalkeeper being introduced as a progression.

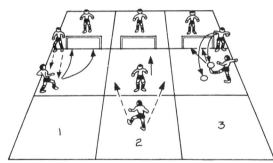

Fig. 52   Drill 2

Drill 3

The players work in groups of 3.

The players shoot at goal while the goalkeeper (gk) performs specific functions. The first player advances on a static goalkeeper, the second player hits a curved ball off a short run-in and the third player attempts to beat an oncoming goalkeeper. The third player has to be especially careful to watch the ball *and* the advancing goalkeeper. He can either drive the ball early or chip it if the goalkeeper commits himself.

Drill 4

The players work in large groups of 8.

A player is fed a number of balls which he approaches at speed from a cone. Depending on which goal he attacks (going for a straight strike or a dribble and shoot move) 2 defenders attempt to close him down.

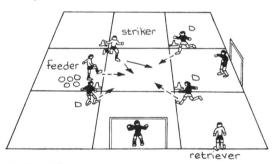

Fig. 54   Drill 4

Drill 5

The players work in groups of 4.

An attacker has to take the ball up to and around the advancing goalkeeper (gk). The players work in 2 pairs, attacking from alternate sides of the grid and swapping the roles of striker and goalkeeper after a set period. The strikers must try to commit the goalkeeper by using disguise. They should also attempt to pass the goalkeeper on his more vulnerable side, that is past his feet, where he has less control.

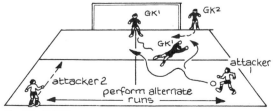

Fig. 55   Drill 5

35

Drill 6

The players work in groups of 8.

This is a 3 v. 3 game, emphasising quick shooting and build-up skills. It is vital to get into a good shooting position but also to be confident enough *not* to shoot when the chances of success are uncertain.

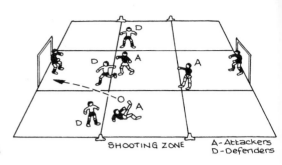

Fig. 56   Drill 6

SHOOTING ZONE

A - Attackers
D - Defenders

HEADING

The skill of heading should not be confined to clearances or shots at goal, since it is also a useful means of passing the ball. It is vital that players in key positions should be skilled in heading because the game is increasingly about converting chances or defending from set-piece plays. Given that many goals result from battles in the air, it obviously pays to practise the skill of heading thoroughly. The speed and athleticism involved in heading make it a unique technique which all outfield players should attempt to master. Young players should be encouraged to enter into controlled heading practices at an early age so that they recognise the great significance of the skill in the game situation.

Strikers are often called upon to make headers as they compete against the opposition's central defenders for a ball crossed in by a team-mate. Other main headers of the ball are wide defenders in broken play or set-pieces and midfield players who are urged to make late attacking runs into the opponents' penalty area. In heading, the timing of the run, the placement of the pass or cross and the power imparted to the ball are just as crucial as the physical size of the target player. Hence success at heading depends as much upon the accuracy of the service as on the receiver's heading technique.

Technical information

To head the ball powerfully a player has to co-ordinate successfully all of the forces involved. The player begins by attacking the ball, that is moving towards it with momentum. The large muscle groups of the legs propel the player upwards and forwards towards the ball. During flight the upper body should work through as large a range of movement as possible so as to generate power at contact. A vigorous double-arm shift is also helpful just before contact is made with the ball on the forehead.

When heading in front of goal you should try to drive high and through the ball towards the target, keeping your head down throughout. For defensive heading try to drive high and up through the ball to clear safely to a team-mate. Experiment with a one or two-legged take-off, a run into the contact point or a straight vertical jump on to the ball, depending on circumstances. The ability to combine a run and a high jump is vital in a crowded goal-mouth, especially if the goalkeeper competes for the ball and has extra reach. Thus practising standing vertical jumps and doing plyometric drills is essential if a player is to develop the necessary elasticity. Football players can learn a great deal by watching high jumpers in the last few strides before take-off, because the techniques employed are similar to those used in heading.

Coaching advice to the player

1.   Use the middle of the forehead for direct, power headers and the side of the forehead for nod-downs or glancing headers. You should

never use the side of the head (temple).
2.   Time your run on to the ball and try and anticipate where the ball will be placed.
3.   Keep your eye on the ball throughout the action.

Advice to coaches

1.   When working with youngsters use light, smooth, plastic balls so as to minimise their fear of injury.

Objectives

1.   To develop defensive and attacking heading skills.
2.   To build an awareness of strategical heading such as the headed pass.

Heading practices

Drill 1

The players work in pairs.
    From a running start a player takes off from one leg, heading the ball back to the hands of his partner. The player retires quickly to the back of the cone which marks the starting-point and repeats the exercise 10 times.

Fig. 57   Drill 1: running header

Drill 2

The players work in pairs as before.
    This time, however, the player heading the

Fig. 58   Drill 2: vertical header

ball makes a vertical jump from both feet. Once again, he heads the ball down into his partner's hands and repeats the exercise 10 times.

Drill 3

The players work in pairs as in the previous 2 drills but this time the player dives to head the ball either to the hands or the feet of his partner. This exercise should be repeated 5 times.

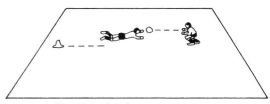

Fig. 59   Drill 3: diving header

Drill 4

The players work in groups of 3.
    The feeder supplies the header with a variety of balls which are then directed past the goalkeeper. The goalkeeper can only react *after* the initial cotnact with the head has been made.

Fig. 60   Drill 4: head for goal

Drill 5

The players work in groups of 4 with 1 ball in play.
    Player 1 throws the ball to player 2 who heads it down to the feet of player 3. Player 3 controls the ball, turns and then throws the ball to player 4, who then heads the ball down to the feet of player 1, and so on.

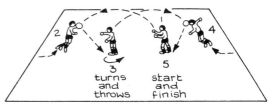

Fig. 61   Drill 5: heading shuttle

Drill 6

This is a 5-a-side practice.
   Player 1 throws the ball to a partner who then attempts to head on to another player who, in turn, catches the ball or gets to it before an opponent. The whole exercise is repeated. Only the heading element is contested.

Fig. 62   Drill 6: head soccer

Drill 7

The players work in groups of 6 (or 8 with opposition).
   Feeders supply 2 players with balls which they head for accuracy and distance to 2 receivers. Opponents to the 2 headers may be added at any stage.

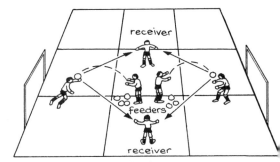

Fig. 63   Drill 7: clearance header

Drill 8

The players work in groups of 4.
   A player heads the ball down to the side while a team-mate sprints into space to receive the knock-down. The exercise is repeated coming back the other way.

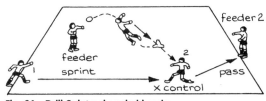

Fig. 64   Drill 8: lateral angled header

GOALKEEPING

It is inevitable that outfield players will make mistakes, miss opportunities to score and execute the occasional poor pass or tackle. However, if they are industrious and concerned about giving a quality performance, they can work hard to make amends for their errors throughout the rest of the match. The one player who is not allowed this luxury is the goalkeeper. He is under continuous pressure and can risk few errors because he is the team's last line of defence. Great keepers are the cornerstones of any side, such that if a team is successful it is invariably because they have a quality goalkeeper behind them. Having an effective and technically skilful goalkeeper in a team instils tremendous confidence in players. Few great sides, both at international and domestic level, have emerged over recent years without having a superb goalkeeper in their midst.
   The skills of the goalkeeper are oriented towards handling and whole body movement. He relies on his speed of reaction, muscular strength, flexibility and agility rather than aerobic capacity and muscular endurance. Therefore the training that a goalkeeper has to be exposed to is highly specific, and should closely resemble those activities which he performs most often in any game. If we conducted a quick performance analysis we

would see that a goalkeeper's main functions are as follows:

- saving shots on goal
- cutting out crosses into the penalty area
- acting as the initial distribution source from certain set-piece and broken play situations
- acting as a general 'marshall' of the defenders in front of him, i.e. he is the principal communicator when the goal is under attack.

Broken down simplistically this means that the goalkeeper's physical work is centred around:

- handling the ball, i.e. catching, deflecting or punching it
- throwing the ball overarm or underarm
- kicking the ball either with a punt or a half-volley
- diving and leaping to intercept shots and crosses
- running, to narrow angles and generally control the shooting zone.

The following sections provide a basic overview of the techniques and skills necessary for effective goalkeeping. For a more detailed breakdown of the many techniques involved in successful goalkeeping, look at *Goalkeeping* by Alex Welsh (A & C Black, 1990).

Stance and ready position. The goalkeeper, on his line, is balanced and alert to any attack

Narrowing the angle head-on. The goalkeeper presents a much bigger obstacle when he comes off his line

Narrowing the angle side-on. The keeper tends the goal from side-on so that both posts can be covered

Stance: the ready position

You should be well balanced at all times so that any type of quick, decisive movement is possible. Flex the legs, bending them slightly so that they are ready for movement, and keep the weight forwards on your toes (you should *not* be flat-footed). Relax the arms and hold them in front of your waist, spreading the fingers to receive the ball. Keep your head steady throughout so as to give you a long, clear view of the advancing ball. With all types of stance the body is well behind the ball.

Positioning for shots at goal

Continually re-adjust your position on or near the goal-line, depending upon the angle to the goal that the attacker takes up as he proceeds to shoot. Ideally, you should bisect that angle so that you are able to cover all eventualities. However, some goalkeepers prefer to move away from this central line to give a little extra protection to their nearest goal-post.

The standing position caters for receiving balls with little speed, while the kneeling position is useful both for dealing with powerful shots and for occasions when the goalkeeper might be unsure of the smoothness of the ground's surface. The combination position is excellent for dealing with bouncing balls because the goalkeeper can either drop or lift his body-weight as necessary.

Narrowing the angle

Wherever possible, you should always seek to come off your line to close down on the shooter and reduce his chances of passing you. This presents a larger obstacle to the striker and reduces the amount of goal that can be seen. Any movement towards the attacker should be swift and you should be watching continually to see if the ball is under control. If it is not, then you should commit yourself totally to the advance so that you can claim the ball; any hesitation can be disastrous in this situation. If the ball is firmly under control, then you should stand firm and tall and remain well balanced in order to move quickly once the shot is executed. This requires great confidence and calmness, and represents the hallmark of a great goalkeeper. The ability to know when to stand firm and entice the advancing player into a hurried shot is a useful means of intimidation,

enabling the goalkeeper to set up a psychological barrier in the mind of the attacker. Thus the goalkeeper can reverse the situation so that the pressure he faces is transferred to the attacker.

You should only advance and go to ground if you really have to. Like the sliding tackle, going to ground to block a shot with your body means that you are totally committed, since you are not likely to recover quickly enough from this position should anything go wrong. Although it is often the easiest and safest way to go to ground, advancing and then sliding out feet first is not acceptable, because it only presents a small obstacle to the oncoming attacker, which he can pass easily. The best body position to adopt is to dive to the ground across the advancing striker, spreading the arms and the legs so as to offer a large body mass which should block any shot. Obviously, this type of technique requires great courage and fine decision-making.

Above all else the goalkeeper must remember not to anticipate what the attacker 'might' do; that would compromise him and jeopardise any psychological advantage he may have had over the shooter. The goalkeeper is a player who constantly has to make critical judgements with little time for contemplation.

Handling shots

Ideally, the goalkeeper should always endeavour to hold on to any shot and grasp it securely to his body. However, in reality we have to understand that, for a variety of reasons, a goalkeeper may be able only to parry or deflect

Handling shots. This is a good body position for when the goalkeeper has time or is receiving a back pass

Handling shots on the ground: the initial position in which the hands hold the ball firmly from behind and on top

Right: correct body position after receiving a waist-high ball which bounced just short of the keeper

Below: receiving head-high shots. Note that the hands are positioned so as to take the weight off the ball

The secondary position where the ball is grasped safely into the body

shots, particularly those that are very strong. In holding on to the ball the goalkeeper effectively ends an attack, while parrying or deflecting the ball still leaves the possibility of another shot from close range occurring. Deflections must, therefore, be pushed out of play and any parried balls need to be claimed with a quick secondary dive.

Ground shots need to be held with the bottom hand slightly behind the ball and the top hand over the ball. Once held the ball should be tucked in closely to the body. If deflected, ground shots should be pushed firmly away with both hands.

Aerial shots need to be held with the hands either side of the ball with the thumbs wrapped behind the ball. Care should be taken on falling to the ground to hold the ball firmly. If deflected, aerial shots should be tipped wide or high over the bar.

Diving and deflecting the ball. Note that the keeper is well spread out with his eyes still on the ball

Dealing with crosses

As well as working well on and around their own goal-line, goalkeepers must also defend the penalty area from ground and aerial crosses. Once again, fine judgement, pin-point positioning, commitment and courage are the

order of the day. This is because the goalkeeper often has to make ground to get to the ball in a crowded penalty area while also keeping his eye on the ball. To be able to have a good view of the ball the goalkeeper has to position himself properly; adopting a central position with an open stance a yard or two off his line is ideal.

Goalkeeping at crosses/corners. Note the body's angle relative to the goal for the ready position, ensuring good vision and movement

Goalkeeping at the near post. Here the keeper demonstrates good leg and hand positioning as he moves in towards the ball

Goalkeeping at the far post. The keeper drives for full extension to meet the ball which is above his head

This enables the keeper to monitor any cross that is placed in front or across him, assessing the power and path (e.g. flat, lofted, curving in, curving out) of the ball. Once this is known, the goalkeeper has to decide whether to expose himself and go for the cross or stay his ground. When he does leave his line he must pick the best path to the ball, which is often around or sometimes through fellow defenders!

High crosses must be taken with outstretched arms, because this gives the goalkeeper a great physical advantage over any potential header of the ball. Also, taking the ball high in its flight-path limits the pressure on the goalkeeper. To take the ball high the keeper has to have a clear run and a powerful single-leg drive at take-off, just as in the high jump. There is a clear summation of forces involved, with the trail leg and the arms driving upwards and forwards to aid lift.

Since most aerial crosses are flung across the goal towards the far post, the goalkeeper has to move out and backwards before he can catch the ball. Technically, this is very difficult and psychologically it can be most disconcerting. In watching the ball the keeper cannot see where he is running, so it pays to take an early glance out and across to see what potential obstacles might crop up. The goalkeeper should wait until he has to leave his goal then go for the ball with full conviction. With a cross to the near post, the goalkeeper's assessment of the ball's flight and his path towards it is much easier.

Handling crosses

As with shots at goal, the goalkeeper should make every effort to hold on to crosses, because panic ensues when a ball is dropped. When a ball cannot be held, usually because of physical

pressure, the goalkeeper must elect to punch or deflect the cross. If a goalkeeper has to punch, he should do so with timing and power. Double-fisted punching is possible when the ball is coming into the goalkeeper but a defender or an attacker is preventing him from going all the way to catch the ball. Single-fisted punching is useful when the goalkeeper has to really stretch backwards for a ball. The arm nearest the opponent protects the ball, while the arm which is goal-side punches the ball away. Deflections should always be pushed away out of play; it is better to concede a corner than to give the opponent a chance at goal.

Distribution from hand and foot

Goalkeepers are the starting-point of any attack. A long kick from the goalkeeper cuts out a number of opponents and places pressure on the opposition's central defenders. If a goalkeeper can punt or half-volley a ball a long distance to a striker who is particularly effective in the air, then he will be a potent attacking weapon for his side.

Another way in which the goalkeeper can initiate an attack is by making a quick clearance, especially if this switches the direction of play. If a goalkeeper intercepts a cross or comes off his line to foil a striker and then immediately initiates an attacking build-up, he is likely to catch the opposition unawares. This is because as opponents push forwards in numbers to score they often leave themselves exposed in

Clearances. The keeper aims for length in his kicking to link with his strikers

A short clearance aimed to accurately reach the feet of the defender correctly weighted

Overarm clearance to a wide receiver. This is a good, accurate and quick method of initiating a new attack

defence. By using the quick throw to distribute to wide receivers in space the goalkeeper can give an attack width and penetration.

If no possibilities for attack are evident, the goalkeeper should wait for his defence to clear their lines before targeting a player and aiming to pass to him, with safety being his primary concern. Usually this means a kick forwards, sometimes executed as a punt, a volley on the run or a half-volley. If the goalkeeper is to be regarded as the first phase of any attack, then he should take great pride in his distribution, just like any outfield player. Accuracy, weighting and timing are just as important to the goalkeeper in his kicking as it is to any creative midfield player. Clearances should be meticulously practised and not seen as a temporary respite before another attacking surge from the opposition.

However, a coach may decide from match analysis that his team's ball retention skills are not good enough from long clearances. In that case the goalkeeper and the back four defenders should look for short, ground-kick clearances which go directly to a player's feet and are easily controlled.

Verbal and non-verbal communication

The goalkeeper has to be in the best position to view the build-up of any attack by the opposition. Thus the goalkeeper can, and must, play a crucial role in 'marshalling his troops' through clear calling (i.e. giving positive advice about what his defenders should do and where they should close down space) and positive non-verbal signalling (i.e. pointing and aggressive gesticulation). This instills confidence in his team-mates and also keeps them informed and on their toes.

Drill 1

The players work in groups of 3.

The goalkeeper is hand-fed ground and aerial 'shots' from a variety of angles.

Fig. 65   Drill 1

Drill 2

The players work in groups of 5.

The goalkeeper has to work intensively to save shots from a variety of angles. The feeders vary the pace and angle of their shots so that the keeper has to continually readjust his position.

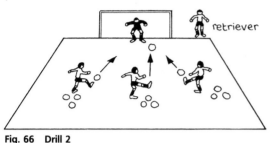

Fig. 66   Drill 2

Drill 3

The players work in groups of 3.

The goalkeeper has to dive and hold shots hit overhead and to either side of him. In the first instance he has to hold a curved shot as soon as it makes contact with the ground. Next he has to hold a ball thrown overhead as soon as it touches the ground. Finally, he repeats the first variation but from the opposite angle. In the first and third variations the keeper has to stay on the near post and step forwards and across.

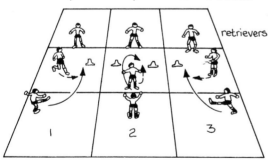

Fig. 67   Drill 3

Drill 4

The players work in pairs.

Fig. 68   Drill 4

Two goalkeepers save a number of 'thrown' shots in sequence. They must throw both aerial and bouncing shots, aiming for power and accuracy.

Drill 5

The players work in pairs.

Two goalkeepers work together, throwing a ball to various positions around the upper body and into the body. The emphasis is on intensive handling.

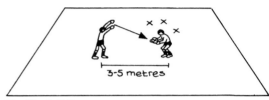

Fig. 69   Drill 5

Drill 6

The players work in groups of 3.

The goalkeeper makes repeated shuttle saves from side to side of a full-sized goal. The feeders provide him with ground and aerial balls alternately. The keeper saves 10 balls before resting. The emphasis should be on making quality saves, holding the ball and bringing it in to the body or deflecting it to safety.

Fig. 70   Drill 6: pressure shuttle

Drill 7

The players work in pairs.

The goalkeeper attempts to 'stand up' in a small-sized goal and save shots driven at him from close range. A possible variation is for the shooter to shout 'Turn' and then hit the ball while the goalkeeper (who stands *facing* the large goal) turns and saves the shot.

The feeder shoots, aiming for a specific target.

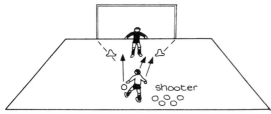

Fig. 71   Drill 7: pressure stand up

Drill 8

The players work in groups of 5.
    The goalkeeper starts at the near post and

only moves when the ball is released from the hands of a feeder. The emphasis is on improving the mobility and positive decision-making of the goalkeeper.

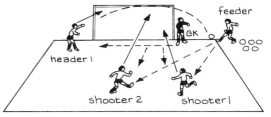

Fig. 72   Drill 8: pressure pull-backs

TEAM SKILLS

Individual skill is vitally important in soccer, but players must realise that they have to compete as a team in order to win matches. It is extremely rare for a player to win a game on his own; statistics show that no individual has enough time on the ball. A striker can turn a match round by making a number of strikes on goal, but even he is dependent upon being given an effective service. Thus we need to think in terms of playing 'units', where groups of players work together to win possession, penetrate defences and either create or close down space in on and off-the-ball situations.
    The ability to create or restrict space when necessary is the hallmark of a good team. Therefore playing units have to set up patterns of play whereby they can gain a numerical advantage over the opposition, for example a 3 v. 2 or 3 v. 1 situation in attack, where the greater the numerical superiority, the greater the attacking potential. Also, they might attempt to overload the midfield in order to dominate possession or push several players forwards to collect the knock-down from a quick, long ball. Finally, outnumbering the opposition in the last third of the pitch always reaps rewards.
    It is implicit in the game of soccer that the player on the ball should not be the only member of a team who is working. However, all too often players do not try hard enough to get

free from their markers in off-the-ball situations. The ball carrier needs to keep his options open and if his team-mates are not prepared to do any unselfish work to make this possible, then the team will not perform to its best. When thinking about how he can help his team, each player should always refer back to the basic principles of play.
    Due to personal physical limitations, the playing environment and the equipment, it is impossible for all 22 players in a game to be actively involved at the same time. Furthermore, since players cannot strike the ball great distances with reasonable accuracy or speed, they tend to cluster around the ball carrier. As a result, any movement made towards the opponents' goal has to be artificially manufactured by means of running with the ball and inter-passing. Thus opponents can be by-passed as players break free from their markers, or they can be eliminated from play by precision passing into space. The most effective size for a unit of players capable of creating such patterns of play is 3 or 4. A 3 v. 3 situation in midfield is not significant until a player gets free or a team-mate from either attack or defence enters, causing a positive overload.
    A player can gain the necessary 'freedom' to offer himself as a potential receiver by the following means:

- pace, i.e. running speed and the ability to accelerate
- deception, i.e. feints and disguises
- agility, i.e. turning, swerving and making angled runs
- physical contact, i.e. pushing off an opponent in a legal challenge for the ball.

These activities might be described as evasive skills.

Earlier, we dealt with the significance of width in attack, with attacking players running wide so as to stretch defences laterally. Good attacking is all about preventing a defensive unit from having any time to become composed. By making telling directional runs on and off the ball, an attacking side can make defenders mark players and space, and if the defence then loses composure they will do neither of these jobs well.

The type of run that the attacking side should perform is conditioned by the area in which the ball is situated and the organisation of the defence. Once again, listing the options proves useful. Thus when the attacking side is on or close to the ball carrier, they can choose any of the following:

- overlapping runs, i.e. sprinting beyond the ball into space
- cross-over runs, i.e. angled runs with a partner across defenders
- diagonal runs, i.e. a precise run across the defence
- dropping-off movements, i.e. short runs into space and away from a tight marker, checking in and out.

Several options are also available when the attacking side is off the ball but the ball carrier has good peripheral vision or an 'awareness' of possible team movement. These are as follows:

- lateral runs to create width
- forward sprints for penetration
- backward movement at pace to offer extra options when no forward movement is possible.

Game situations involving directional running

Overlapping runs

1. With this simple overlapping run it is not

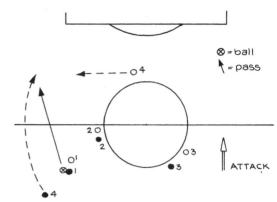

Fig. 73   A possible game situation involving directional running

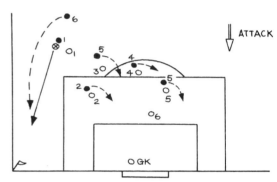

Fig. 74   Overlapping runs (1)

possible to pass the ball in the immediate playing area.
2.   Here there is the possibility of an overlapping run for a wide midfield player or a wide defender, as the attackers are checking to go away from defenders into space.

Cross-over runs

1.   A wide defender (3) makes a cross-over run and takes the ball down the line before making a cross into the penalty area.

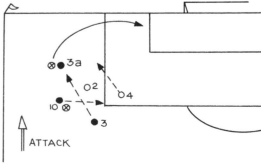

Fig. 75   Overlapping runs (2)

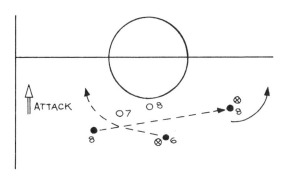

Fig. 76　Cross-over runs (1)

2. 2 midfield players make flat runs across each other's paths in order to change the direction of the attack. Midfield player 6 shows the ball to player 8 so that he can hide the ball and then sprint away with it after the cross-over.

Diagonal runs

1. A central striker (9) makes a diagonal run across the defence into space out wide, while

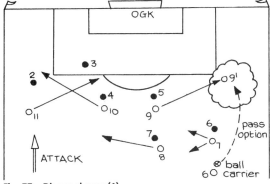

Fig. 77　Diagonal runs (1)

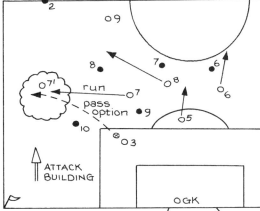

Fig. 78　Diagonal runs (2)

other players take defenders away to give him room and to prepare for the ensuing cross.
2. An attacking player (7) makes an angled run to give the defender the option of counter-attacking when he retrieves the ball.

Reverse/forward movement

A wide attacker (11) makes a decoy movement at the same time as a striker (10) makes an angled run down the line to receive the ball from a throw. The striker then drops forwards into space to control the ball.

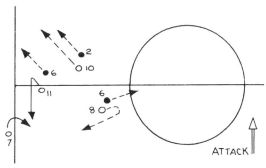

Fig. 79　Reverse/forward movement

Forward/turn/sprint sequence

A striker (10) makes a decoy movement and then sprints into space. He continues sprinting and waits for the ball to reach him.

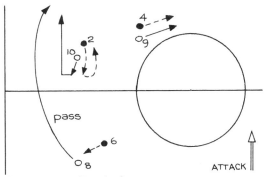

Fig. 80　Forward/turn/sprint sequence

Directional running practices

Drill 1

This is a 3 v. 2 situation where the free player attempts to make telling runs into space behind

47

the defenders. The aim is to encourage well-timed overlapping runs, with the player always being active.

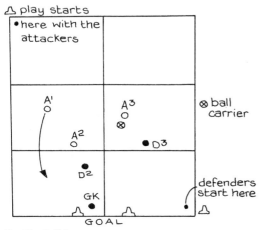

Fig. 81   Drill 1

Drill 2

This is a 2 v. 2 situation with receivers only being available in a certain sector of the grid. The aim here is to get the 2 attackers to beat the defenders on their own by using deception. The receivers should only be used as a last resort.

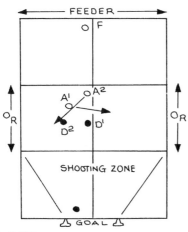

Fig. 82   Drill 2

Drill 3

This is a 3 v. 3 situation in which the players attempt to find space by making angled runs. When the players gain the ball in space they should try to carry the ball to one of the cones

placed on the outside of the training grid. The run by player 3 is particularly telling because it goes on the blind side, behind defender 2 who is nearest.

Drill 4

This is a 3 v. 3 practice in a short, wide playing area. It emphasises the need for support runs which are correctly timed and angled. It is important for the players to communicate and for them to have the confidence to release the ball at the right moment and weight the pass correctly. Supporting players should be active throughout so as to upset the balance of the defence.

Drill 5

This is a 5 v. 5 practice with sides attacking or defending 2 goals. The attackers make penetrative diagonal runs to drag the defence out of position. They also make rapid changes of direction to find space, that is they 'load' an area of the grid and then break out. Note that there is no goalkeeper in this practice.

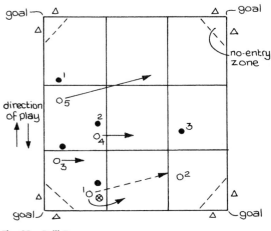

Fig. 83   Drill 5

Drill 6

This is a 4-a-side practice in which players try to attack unmarked small goals, using space and width and keeping the ball under control. Each team attacks for 5 minutes. When an attack breaks down the ball is returned to the feeder and the practice restarts.

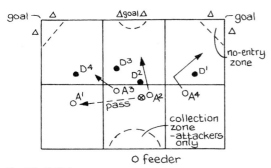

Fig. 84 Drill 6

Drill 7

This is a 4 v. 3 situation. The thrower joins the action after putting the ball in play. The attacking players check in and out rapidly and at different times. The defenders aim to keep play tight to the side-lines.

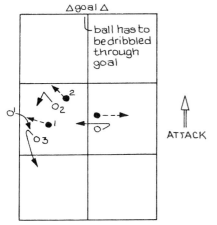

Fig. 85 Drill 7

Passing

The previous practices emphasised the importance of the initial movement of players around the ball carrier. Clearly, to be completely successful the ball carrier has to execute his pass correctly, which brings into question the importance not only of directional running but also directional passing, and the ways in which penetration can be achieved by particular passing patterns. Ball speed is a vital component in the development of close passing routines, because quick, short passes can often create space which defenders cannot cover due to

their inability to react in time. Also, long forward passes maintain the forward momentum of an attack, while in certain passing manoeuvres such as the wall pass the strategical placement of players directly in front of defenders can isolate an opponent effectively.

As has been already mentioned, the timing, accuracy and weighting of a pass are absolutely critical in the creation of space. When moving into small-sided practices and full games it also becomes important for each player (and the team as a whole) to develop good vision. An individual's peripheral vision, that is the extent of his visual field, can be enhanced if he is encouraged to watch other players as well as the ball; this will also enable him to anticipate his opponents' movements. Great passers of the ball scan the action prior to receiving or releasing a ball. They have the unique ability of being able to scrutinise the action quickly and then choose the correct option.

The wall pass

The wall pass is very effective, especially in and around the opposition's penalty area or when an attacking player backs on to a defender to take him out of the action. In the last third of the pitch, or in closed-down positions (for example near to the sides of the pitch) where defenders are often static, the wall pass makes it possible for space to be exploited quickly. In these situations time is at a premium, so the wall pass, with its explosive change of pace and subtle angled returns, is an ideal passing option.

The wall pass is literally a pass which bounces quickly back into space off the feet of the receiver. It requires a first-time touch from the receiver as the initial ball carrier will be moving at pace and expecting a crisp return. However, one note of caution is necessary: if there is not a certain amount of disguise from the incoming dribbler, and the distance between the players is too close, then an interception is likely. If executed properly, defenders should not have time to adapt and therefore, ideally, the attacker performing the assist to the ball carrier should be less than 10 metres (or yards) away. The player does not have to remain static (unless he wants to commit his own defender), so he can move in a couple of metres to create the best line or angle for the ensuing wall pass. The basic execution of the wall pass is shown in figs. 86 and 87.

Implicit within the wall passing technique is

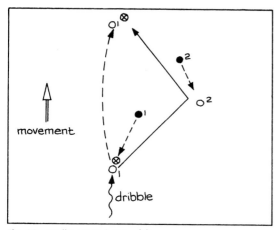

Fig. 86 Wall pass technique (1)

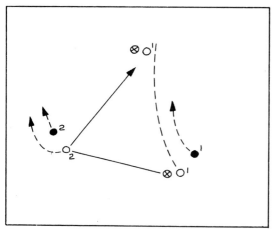

Fig. 87 Wall pass technique (2)

speed, that is player speed, ball speed and speed of thought and action. The higher the level of football a player aspires to, then the greater the likelihood that this type of passing will become commonplace. It is often the only way that space can be found in competitive or defence-orientated matches.

Playing 2 and 1 touch soccer in small-sided training sessions (as in the following practices) is an excellent way of testing accuracy, alertness and physical fitness. The practices demand great skill in shielding, deception and disguise on the ball, and also enhance vision, communication and team co-ordination. At worst, the practices will expose any technical, tactical or conditioning inadequacies in footballers.

Wall pass practices

Drill 1

An angled pass out is made by an attacker. The 2 defenders remain relatively static in the early learning stages. The ball carrier should attempt to disguise his intentions, and for both the attackers, especially the supporting player, an explosive change of pace is essential. The dribbling player must try to bring the tackler on to him.

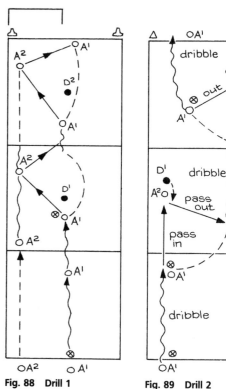

Fig. 88   Drill 1   **Fig. 89   Drill 2**

Drill 2

A lateral pass out is made against 2 defenders operating a tight marking system. The emphasis here is on the timing of the pass and the angle of run necessary to retain the ball by dribbling.

Drill 3

This is a dummied wall pass which attempts to decieve the defender by means of a step-over or similar disguise. The disguise is carried out by

50

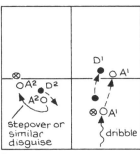

Fig. 90 Drill 3

the 'rebound' player (A) who tries to confound defender 2. This practice emphasises the importance of improvisation, peripheral vision and the execution of the manoeuvre at pace.

Drill 4

Dribbler A^1 makes a dummy wall pass to a team-mate, A^2, to drag defender 2 into a 'possible' interception, before driving away in the opposite direction at speed. D^1 'buys' the dummy and goes for an interception. The important thing here is that the deception should be plausible enough to take in the defenders.

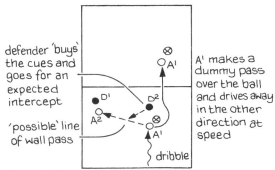

Fig. 91 Drill 4

Long passes

The previous practices concentrated on short passes hit with absolute accuracy and the correct weight. Other passing and movement patterns centre around the long pass, which may be lofted, curved (inswing and outswing) or hit along the ground. These types of pass all take defenders out of the game momentarily, and if they are coupled with superb angled running from team-mates into the space behind the defence, the final results can be devastating. Clearly, these passes are open to interception because they travel longer and take more time

to reach their destination. However, the subtlety of the curved pass, drifting as it does away from defenders, is its great virtue, and a long ball hit diagonally across defence finds space due to the fact that play and attention is concentrated near to the actual ball carrier.

When coupled with delayed or blind-side runs from players on the opposite flank to the immediate action, these types of pass can disrupt defences. Obviously, they require great confidence on the part of the passer, because it can be all too easy to throw away possession. Nevertheless, the potential rewards justify the risk, for the switch from defence to attack is so swift that many defenders will be left stranded or simply unable to cope as the ball travels across and beyond them. Defences like to be able to regroup and backtrack to the edge of their own penalty area while their midfield players delay and contain the opposition's advance. Long balls which are hit by the opposition when the defence least expects it do not allow the comfort of any such preparation.

Limited touch soccer practices

Drill 1

This is a 3 v. 3 situation in which players are allowed to touch the ball either 2 or 3 times. The emphasis is on ensuring a good first control, and the player should have the confidence to look for an early forward passing opportunity. The player must also be confident enough *not* to touch the ball but to let it run freely. Running off the ball should be at a maximum for penetration.

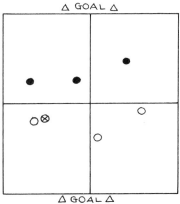

Fig. 92 Drill 1

Drill 2

This is a 6-a-side situation involving goalkeepers. Players may touch the ball 1 or 2 times. This drill emphasises the need to create space and exploit width for penetration as a unit. If the unit cannot go forwards they should go across or even back, but they must hang on to the ball. Thus a great deal of patience is required in carrying out this drill.

As a progression, the 'pitch' could be narrowed so as to make it even harder for the players to find space.

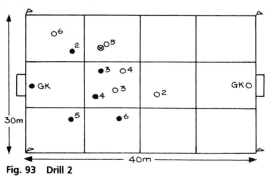

Fig. 93   Drill 2

Passing cycles

Drill 1

This is a 2 v. 2 situation with 4 free receivers available for use as rebound targets for either pair. The aims are to make a large number of consecutive plays and to create great variety in passing in order to disrupt the opposition.

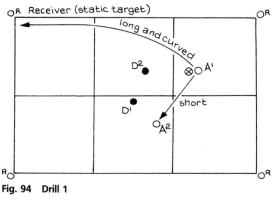

Fig. 94   Drill 1

Drill 2

This is a 2 v. 2 situation as before but this time the receivers are mobile. The emphasis is on long passing coupled with active support to ensure that possession is maintained. Passes are hit to receivers with space and a target in mind. The length of the drill may depend on the number of consecutive passes made or on the length of cycles of play (i.e. 30 seconds and ball retention).

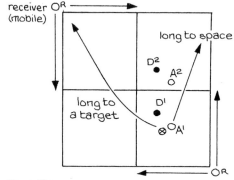

Fig. 95   Drill 2

Long passing practices

Drill 1

This is a 4 v. 2 situation with players separated by a no-go zone. 4 attackers attempt to keep the ball from 2 defenders who move about between zones when the ball is transferred. The emphasis is on peripheral vision and making intuitive passes for length. The players should change roles often for variety.

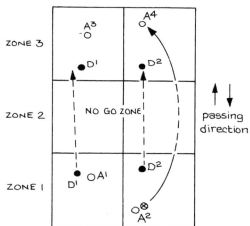

Fig. 96   Drill 1

Summary

Successful soccer teams have to be skilled in the whole range of passing techniques. They must also be able to find space and gaps in defences by ingenious running on and off the ball. Indeed, these two components of play have to be co-ordinated to reap the maximum rewards. Similarly, the skills must be viewed in context; for example if little time is left and your side is losing, then the key decision-makers have to gamble on the most direct route to goal (a 1 or 2-pass routine) or be confident that they can still build a viable attack.

Thus successful sides are those who are able to do the following:

- win high balls
- retain possession
- continually probe for weaknesses
- improvise
- take the initiative
- work well both as a team and as separate units, i.e. defence, midfield, attack.

SET-PIECE SITUATIONS

Statistics show that nearly 50% of all goals scored come from 'dead ball' situations. It seems strange, therefore, that teams do not devote more care and planning to the practice of set-piece play.

When we examine the rules which condition the nature of set-piece plays, we can see that there are built-in advantages for the attacking team (e.g. the opposition must be 10 metres (or yards) away at free kicks, and the ball is motionless). The attacking side can also pack the penalty area with players to cause maximum disturbance or help execute a planned move. Set-piece plays do not have to be very complex, and often the key is efficiency in timing, accuracy and disguise. Space does not permit any detailed analysis of each set-piece situation, but the following common coaching points are worth noting.

- Make sure that you and your team-mates are ready before executing the free kick or throw.
- Establish some sort of visual or verbal code for set-piece ploys.
- Make sure that key play-makers are on the ball in the relevant instances (i.e. the most powerful player with good shoulder mobility ought to take the long throw-ins).
- Utilise all of your physical (height) and technical (striking a curved ball) skills to your best advantage.
- Shoot directly at goal wherever possible.

- Look for 'rebounds' and get attacking players into the 6-yard box as often as possible.
- Try to vary corner kicks. For example, you could hit a short corner kick to a player on the near post, who then flicks on the ball to a team-mate.
- Try to have 2 play-makers ready on the ball where possible; this will leave you with more options, and will make disguise easier.
- When a defensive wall appears use your own players to disrupt their vision or route to the ball (i.e. place men in front/side/behind the wall).
- Use long throws into the penalty area when possible.
- Throw forwards into space whenever possible, so that the receiver has a good chance of controlling the ball.

Game restarts like throw-ins are vastly underrated as far as their attacking potential goes. In fact, 5 in every 100 goals come direct from throw-ins.

Defending at set-piece plays is really all about organisation, that is marking tightly, closing down space, and attacking the potential striker or receiver of the ball. Thus the defence could cut off a throw-in or a corner kick to an attacking player at the near post by positioning a player in front of and behind him. This requires quick thinking, prompt action and careful organisation so that no other gaps are left. This is when a good goalkeeper comes into his own, because he is the one who marshalls the defence and dictates defensive options. In defence, all players must concentrate and communicate with each other in order to quickly seal off any danger. If they do this then they will concede very few goals from set-piece plays.

Free kicks

Direct free kick

There are 2 possible strikers of the ball and therefore they can disguise their intentions. The attacking wall breaks up to reveal the target zone and a player is positioned on either side to deal with rebounds.

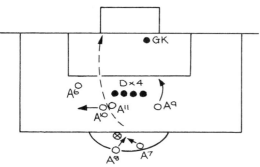

Fig. 97   Direct free kick

Indirect free kick

There are 2 initial passers and 2 possible strikers at goal or feeders into the penalty area. Late and early runs into the penalty area make several aerial and ground options available.

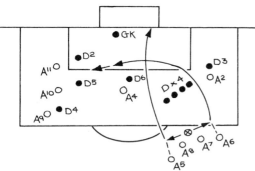

Fig. 98   Indirect free kick

Corner kicks

Outswinger

The ball goes away from the goalkeeper and into the path of oncoming headers.

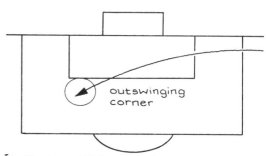

Fig. 99   Corner kick (outswinger)

Inswinger

The ball is hit directly to an attacker who can outjump the defence from a static position or make effective runs into the box.

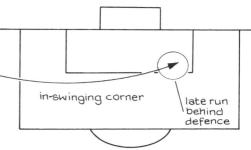

Fig. 100   Corner kick (inswinger)

Short pass and cross

This practice makes use of the fact that defenders have to be 10 metres (or yards) away from the ball at a corner.

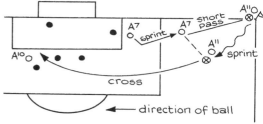

Fig. 101   Short pass and cross routine at a corner kick

Near post flick-on

An accurate feed is necessary for this practice. The attacking side makes use of their taller players.

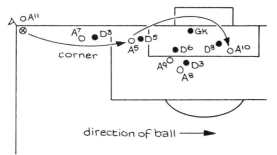

direction of ball ⟶

Fig. 102 Near post flick-on at a corner kick

Throw-ins

Into the box

The aerial throw may be used here for an attacker to head on, control and turn or lay off to a team-mate.

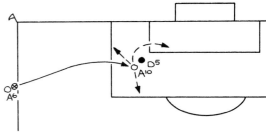

Fig. 103 Throw-in into the box

Into space

With good decoy running the player can throw the ball forwards into space or at the feet of a team-mate (or both).

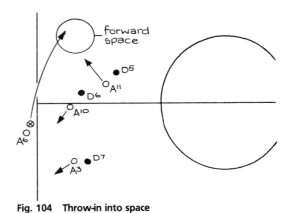

Fig. 104 Throw-in into space

PRINCIPLES OF PLAY

Even teams like Liverpool, whose players are unafraid of taking risks, take account in their game planning and tactical preparations of particular 'principles of play' which influence the way individual players and the team as a whole perform. Soccer players have an enormous amount of information to process if they are to be successful in a match situation. While performing according to an assigned role, the footballer also has to continually assimilate information about the ball in play, the space he is guarding and the work of his team-mates and his opponents. He can do this in an off or an on-the-ball situation, in a particular area of the field and within a specified period.

Soccer experts can study the behaviour of players in games to see if there are particular trends or principles of play which underpin a team's performance and have a bearing on the success of match tactics. Thus coaches and scientists can use set game situations to examine objectively the individual and collective skills of a team and to decide how victory can best be achieved.

Attacking principles

In soccer, a team wins by scoring more goals than the opposition, and to do that the defensive zone must be penetrated in order to create shooting opportunities. It is possible that extremely gifted footballers can perform this task on their own, but usually even they require assistance from team-mates, with goals resulting from pre-defined moves. In the first instance, possession has to be secured and then retained. Next, the team has to make inroads into the opposition's half and penetrate their penalty area. In some matches this forward progress can be very hard and a war of attrition can develop, particularly if both sides are highly combative in midfield. On other occasions teams can freely give up the middle ground to their opponents and prepare for an attack by grouping compactly within the final defensive third, thus effectively restricting space in that area of the pitch where it is at a premium (time and space in the penalty area mean goal-scoring chances).

Width

The first principle of play for the attack is that of width. By moving forwards on a broad front the attacking side has more space in which to perform. The crucial factor is not necessarily the work of the ball carrier but the running and positioning of his team-mates off the ball. All too often players offer themselves short and close, thinking that they are providing valuable support when all they are doing in reality is to restrict play and allow one defender to cover two attackers. Also, if they come in too close there will only be a limited amount of preparation time for ball reception and a minimum of space to work in. Thus attacks should spread out across and in front of the ball carrier so that the defence has to make awkward decisions as to whether to mark space or the incoming player. Width in attack also stretches a defence physically and makes them

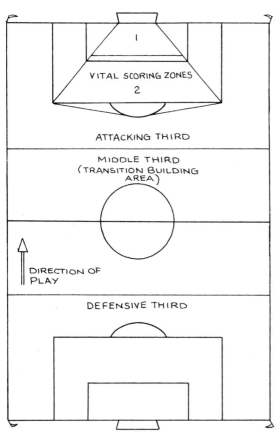

Fig. 105   Areas of play on a soccer pitch

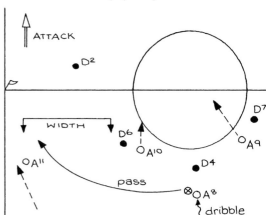

Fig. 106   A¹¹ offers A⁸ the best option by producing width in attack

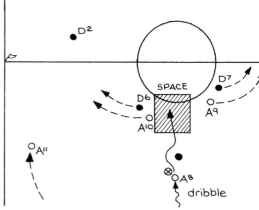

Fig. 107   A¹⁰ and A⁹ help take defenders away and offer a space behind the primary defender

run more to close down space. It offers the ball carrier greater choice in that he might see space beyond his primary defender and decide to attack that player, exploiting the gaps by running with the ball. Thus, a player may do a great deal of damage by his use of creative movement off the ball. What his running serves to do is to disperse the cover behind the primary defender.

Support

The second attacking principle is that of support. When building an attack the ball carrier has to be supported by one or two players who come from behind the line of the ball and help penetrate space while also presenting the defenders with additional problems. If the defence has to watch the ball while this occurs then a chance is being created by the supporting runners. One problem arising with the principles of width and support is that if the move breaks down the intitial attacking side will have left gaps behind them which can then be breached. Therefore as attacks build width and support for the ball carrier, the deep defenders in the same team must watch the spaces in front of and around them and be prepared to act promptly. This scenario explains why midfield players can do so much work (11,000–12,000 metres (12,000–13,000 yards) in 90 minutes), because balls are lost in midfield and because they perform many supporting runs to get ahead of and then behind the ball.

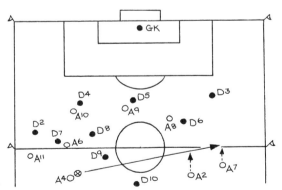

Fig. 108   A ball has just been won. By running, A² and A⁷ give the ball carrier an option to create width

Depth

Another crucial principle of attack is depth. This means that if play does break down or is held

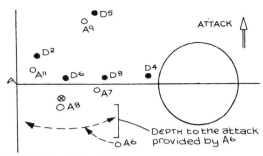

Fig. 109   Depth in attack

up, then a player is in close proximity and can help immediately.

Mobility

Coupled with the notion of supportive forward runs is the need to develop a principle of mobility in attack. This means that more deeply positioned attackers can do valuable work by becoming 'perpetual motion' footballers, moving freely and seemingly randomly across defences in an attempt to disconcert opponents.

Strikers can be the most inactive of players in terms of work-rates, sometimes spending up to 60% of their time walking, resting or performing non-purposive work. But their contribution is vital, and to emphasise this point effectively, a coach only has to track a striker with a video for a game and then replay it, pointing out his work-rate and the positive or negative spin-off it has for the rest of the team.

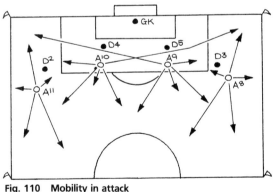

Fig. 110   Mobility in attack

Penetration

However, the ultimate principle for all players when an attack is in full flow is penetration, whereby the attack seeks to make fatal incisions into the heart of a defence with the sole objective of scoring a goal. The actions open to

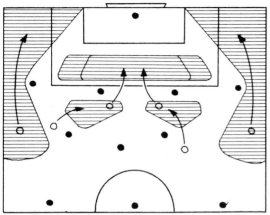

Fig. 111 The dangerous spaces, i.e. space behind and around defences, where dribblers and runners without the ball must penetrate

each player in an attack relate to their individual technical prowess, notably their dribbling, passing and running skills. Obviously in match situations this comes down to face-to-face confrontation, as in striker versus central defender, or wide midfielder against wide defender. The link between winning individual battles and the final team result is what makes soccer so fascinating and absorbing to the expert coach or sports scientist. By careful goal setting a coach can get a player to concentrate totally on winning his 'mini-match' against his opponent. In training, the 1 v. 1 situation represents the game in microcosm.

Without question the most important skill in relation to building individual and team penetration is dribbling. Being able to drift past defenders and move into space behind defences is tactically indispensable to a team. Players who can dribble the ball are the true creators in a side, and if they also display good aerobic fitness then the coach should tap this rare talent to the full. Thus a coach could investigate where space is likely to exist in a defence and get these types of player to probe that territory. This space may well exist wide on the flanks and behind the two wide defenders, or in front of the central defence if the strikers have done their work in dragging their markers wide. Either way great dribblers should be nurtured by the coach and encouraged to attack defences. These players often portray great virtuosity when on the ball, providing skills and touches which even the greatest defenders would find difficult to counteract. Indeed, such novelty and improvisation should be promoted by the coach for they offer a team that quality which

opponents cannot plan against, that is the unexpected. However, it is important that these virtuoso players show their own team-mates what they have planned and where they plan to execute it on the pitch, otherwise support might not be available if things go wrong!

Defensive principles

The objectives of any sound defence will be the exact opposite of those of an attacking unit, that is to prevent goals (obtain a 'shut out' or 'clean sheet'), to minimise penetration, to regain possession and to have an active defence which pushes the opposition further away from the vital scoring zone. Individual defence is possible just as in individual attacking flair, but defence is best viewed as a corporate or unit skill. This is not to deny the significance of skills such as tackling, marking, containing, covering, intercepting and channelling, but simply to place greater emphasis on group solidarity, because errors made in defence, whether technical or tactical, can be critical (i.e. goals are scored), whereas in attack possession can be regained if things break down. Defensive work is generally centred around the periphery of the penalty area, so slip-ups by defenders here offer little chance for recovery, and the marshalling of defensive players is vital.

As with attack, there are principles for sound defence. Before discussing these in detail it is worth noting that a defender needs to possess the personal qualities of composure, patience and concentration when on the pitch.

Delay

Play is conducted in front of the defence on most occasions, or at least the build-up or setting-up of an attack unfolds before a defender. The objective of the attacking side is to get beyond that defence; the defender's role is one of negating any forward movement, or slowing down the process. Delay is, therefore, a major defensive principle, but it must be viewed positively as a necessary but temporary time-lag before possession is regained. The crucial factors are when, where and how the defender achieves this, and they explain why individual defenders must have high levels of self-discipline and sound decision-making skills in order to make the challenge to repossess a timely one.

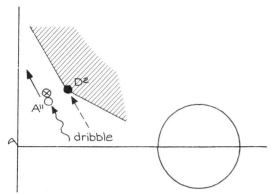

Fig. 112 Delay in defence through containment and restriction

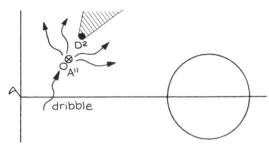

Fig. 113 A bad example of defending, allowing the attacker time and space

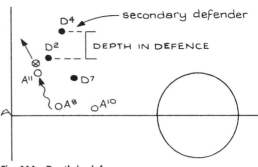

Fig. 114 Depth in defence

The primary defender, that is the player who is nearest the ball when possession is lost and the opposition look to attack, has to limit the ball carrier, curbing his passing or running opportunities. By moving towards the ball carrier and, therefore, involving himself in active defence, he closes down the playing space. If an attacker is moving forwards at speed, then he needs to be closed down quickly or channelled away from the scoring zone whenever possible. This is referred to as 'jockeying' and would involve a structured containment rather than an initial tackle.

Given that defences function as a unit, the secondary defender needs to be involved near the ball. His proximity to the ball carrier and primary defender depends upon where the action is on the pitch. If it is near to the defence's own goal area, then the secondary defender would push close and attempt to cover, while also trying to mark another attacker. In midfield, where pressure is less intense, the secondary defender might slide in at an angle behind the immediate play so as to give physical depth to the defence.

Thus the principle of depth is multi-faceted in its practical significance. Firstly, the secondary

defender closes off attacking space behind the primary defender, giving that player confidence. This confidence can be reaffirmed verbally simply by telling the primary defender of his presence. Also, directional cues and advice can be shouted to the primary defender, which is often disconcerting to the ball carrier in that he sees and hears his options fading away. If a challenge regains the ball, then the secondary defender is close enough to sprint ahead or alongside the new ball carrier to swiftly turn defence into attack, creating a springboard for penetration. Thus in midfield, that is the preparation or transition area of the pitch, the secondary defender tries to squeeze possible attacking space and provide valuable psychological and technical support. In set-piece situations, he is forced to move to a one-to-one marking situation, especially at corners or free kicks which drift into the penalty area, where no possible attacker can be allowed space or time.

To counteract any side which can switch the direction of play and which possesses attacking mobility, the defence has to have a certain equilibrium. Defences invariably pivot around the two central defenders, depending on whether play is on the left or right flank. The danger is that too many defenders can go to offer the primary defender support and so get dragged out of a covering position. If a rapid change of direction then took place, the defence would be penetrated easily because of this ineffective loading. However, on some occasions, for example a direct free kick on the edge of the penalty box, a defence *would* load the area. In this situation every player would be called back so as to pick up individual opponents and effectively deny the attacker any ground space. This does mean that an aerial attack has greater potential for success, but hopefully the defending team's goalkeeper will take command of any balls in flight.

Balance

Attacking mobility seeks to create a numerical imbalance whereby defenders are confronted with several opponents. Deep defenders, therefore, have to be ever-alert, even if the ball is not near them, so that no sudden, long, diagonal pass finds them over-exposed. Thus the final defensive principle is one of physical balance.

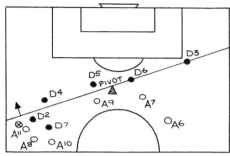

Fig. 115 Defenders 6 and 3 provide the defence with depth and balance

TACTICS AND DECISION-MAKING

Tactics are an important part of the game of soccer and they give particular meaning to the nature of team performance. In essence, tactics are the underlying ideas and strategic thoughts which make sense of everything individual players or teams do during competition. Tactics determine the extent to which a team utilises its range of soccer skills, and are also closely linked to the extent to which a coach tries to contain the play of the opposition. All too often the tactics that a team employs are born out of knowledge of the opposition and their key players. Tactics should be built around the team's own strengths, that is all those individual and unit skills which will help the team gain power and control in a match. In soccer this comes down to:

■ winning individual duels, especially to gain possession
■ controlling areas of the field of play, for example the midfield
■ applying pressure in set-pieces and re-starts
■ dominating certain phases of the match, for example either side of half-time or the last quarter of the match.

Having an awareness of team tactics allows us to look at soccer performance in an objective manner. For example a number of factors need to be considered when a coach decides what the tactics for a particular game will be. These include:

■ the technical strengths of his side
■ the physical preparation of each player
■ the psychological readiness of both individuals and the team
■ the style of play of the opposition
■ the tactics they have used in previous matches
■ the playing environment (surface, weather, etc.)
■ the type of encounter (friendly, cup, league match) and the importance of the outcome to players and club (promotion/relegation).

All of these factors are interrelated, but the coach must give priority to some of them.

Pressure

In élite soccer performance, for example at national level or in the English First Division, a manager cannot expect his players to dominate a match for a full 90 minutes. Every team will be placed under pressure at some point in a match and, realistically, a manager must hope that his team copes well and rides the storm without conceding a goal. What any team at any level should endeavour to do is to win as many individual tactical battles as possible. Also, they should aim to maximise the spells of pressure they apply, and convert this pressure into goals or at least territorial supremacy. To do this each player should be encouraged to think positively during the game, constantly picking up information and cues and responding quickly either to danger or to attacking opportunities. They also should be interacting throughout with their team-mates, talking and praising each other and being positive rather than negative in their feedback. Coaches must be aware of the fact that the higher the standard of a competition is, the more closely contested it is likely to be.

Decision-making

Another factor which seriously affects a team's chances of success is their on-the-field capacity to make decisions, and especially the strategic decisiveness of their key play-makers. It is an important point for all coaches and managers to remember that, at the end of a week's preparation for a match, all the coach can do is sit in the dug-out or stand. We may see on the television professional managers and coaches watching and shouting anxiously from their vantage point, but they are in effect relatively powerless to affect the state of play in a match. True, they can substitute players and supply an encouraging, motivating team talk at half-time, but apart from these moments the game has to take its course. Thus coaches and managers should foster situations in practice which encourage players to think and make positive decisions about game play.

Match analysis

Coaches might also consider designing 'clinics' where the player's strategical awareness is taken to a higher level. Thus they might use video observation and analysis to give feedback on aspects of the game such as ball retention, scoring from set-piece plays, or an individual player's on-the-ball action. Over time, comparisons of individual or team performance can be made, and the coach can help instill within his players the feeling that game

awareness and positive decision-making form a process that they can build on together. Through studying videos or statistics of their own performances, players will soon realise that the opportunities for ball control are few (i.e. the on-the-ball time is approximately 90 seconds per 90 minutes), and that moments on the ball have to be used to the full in relation to overall game strategy. Thus, for example, the fact that in the 1982 World Cup over 80 of the 126 goals were scored from passing cycles of 4 passes or less, might be used to emphasise the importance of key players who can control games by their skills or thinking.

Play-makers and team tactics

Once he has identified a key player, the coach should ensure that he is given a lot of the ball at the right time and in the right place on the field. Furthermore, he should create support systems that provide the player with the physical freedom to express his talents.

Every player should know the team's game plan or match tactics, and thus coaches and players need to spend a considerable amount of time together, talking and sharing ideas. There is great value to be had in investing power and trust in players, particularly the key decision-makers. These players need to be located close to the action and in other strategical positions on the pitch (e.g. wide on the flanks) where they can attack opponents and manoeuvre into space.

In soccer, coaches generally look to subsume the individual into the 'team', such that key individuals invariably become totally subservient to the overriding game plan. Coaches need to evaluate how rigidly players must adhere to a particular system of play, because there is a danger of producing a stereotypical, bland kind of football. Tactics should seek to exploit the whole range of physical and technical skills that a team possesses. They should be flexible so that play-makers can initiate change when a particular approach is not succeeding. In soccer, decision-making is an on-going process and the reason why teams like Liverpool have remained so successful is that they take to the field with a positive attitude, completely confident in their own individual and collective ability to manipulate events as necessary.

THE PHYSICAL REQUIREMENTS OF THE GAME

In soccer today there is a growing interest in the physical preparation of players and some professional clubs are becoming much more precise in the nature of their physical training. Soccer performance is a product of all physical and mental characteristics of the individual. Of course, some of these factors are determined at birth, for example somatotype (body shape), height and age. Thus for goalkeeping physical size is of paramount importance but, due to the specific demands placed upon the keeper, age seems *not* to be an overriding factor.

Endurance

Endurance is a vital component in the performance of every soccer player. It can be broken down into two elements: aerobic endurance and local muscular endurance. The following table helps to place our understanding of these elements in a soccer context.
Clearly, these two types of endurance capability are linked and soccer needs both components in abundance since it involves both prolonged bouts of jogging and striding, and moments of high-energy sprinting with active recovery.

Aerobic endurance

Aerobic simply means working 'with air', that is taking in, transporting and utilising oxygen. A soccer player's 'aerobic capacity' (VO_2 max), is the maximum volume of oxygen which he can utilise per minute. Aerobic endurance relates to the ability of a player to sustain light to moderately hard physical exercise over a long period of time. The cardio-respiratory system (lungs, heart and blood vessels) supplies the muscles with oxygen, and allows the 'freeing' of muscle fuels for aerobic and anaerobic work. Soccer is a sport which requires a good endurance base because of the length of time of the competition (at least 90 mins), the distance players run (10,000–11,000+ metres) (11,000–12,000+ yards)) and the varied nature of the runs (i.e. a mixture of jogging, striding, sprinting and brisk walking). Also, having a sound endurance base in a footballer's training regime will enable other physical fitness components like strength and speed to be conditioned more effectively. However, soccer coaches and players structuring their own fitness training must remember that it is no good having a tremendous transport system for delivering oxygen to the working muscle(s) if the muscles themselves have a poor endurance

Type of endurance	Activity	Physiological demands
Aerobic	Prolonged work, demonstrating the footballer's ability to engage in continuous physical activity and offset fatigue.	Taking in, transporting and using oxygen.

Type of endurance	Activity	Physiological demands
Muscular	The capacity of a muscle or group of muscles to engage in continuous physical work.	Local muscular fatigue or muscular exhaustion.

capability. Thus local muscular endurance is vital if a player is to make maximum use of the oxygen his muscles receive.

Muscular endurance

In order to cope with the large volumes of oxygen which are needed during lengthy exercise, muscles have to be trained to use the oxygen more efficiently and to offset muscular fatigue. Training increases the number of muscle capillaries per square millimetre of muscle area and this will ensure an increased blood flow to the working muscle. This particular type of training is referred to as **overload** taining. What happens is that the muscle groups are made to work repeatedly over the same range of movement, resistance, speed and frequency as they would in a match. The functional effect on the muscle will be increased utilisation of muscle capillaries and muscle fibres (motor units), and the improved removal of the metabolic waste products (carbon dioxide and lactic acid) which result from physical activity.

Local muscular endurance relates to a player's ability to sustain a quality performance while undertaking highly strenuous physical work.

Anaerobic endurance

Much of a soccer player's work is of a long term, aerobic nature, but he will be faced with physical demands which require short term or anaerobic endurance.

Anaerobic simply means working without air. This type of endurance can be sustained only for short periods and is invariably an addition to the aerobic structure, utilised when a muscle cannot cope with certain physical work demands by means of the aerobic system alone. Thus in soccer anaerobic work might be necessary at the start of a match (especially if the player has not warmed up properly), during explosive movements such as leaping to head a ball or diving to tip a shot over the bar, and when a player is asked to engage in intensive all-out bouts of activity, for example when a striker makes a series of sprints and chases for the ball. What is happening is that other resources/fuels are being called into play in the muscle because of a lack of oxygen, enabling anaerobic work periods of 0–10 seconds or 10–30 seconds, depending upon the intensity of the activity.

Fatigue

Fatigue is a term which is used a great deal but it is rarely understood or defined properly. For the purposes of a discussion of fatigue in soccer I would define the term as 'The deterioration, physical and psychological, that occurs when a soccer player engages in and continues to engage in a physical activity/skill.' In soccer, a player may experience localised fatigue in those muscles constantly in use, or a more general fatigue resulting from extreme demands made on the player's energy reserves over a short space of time. However, it should not be forgotten that some players can tolerate the psychological effects of fatigue better than others.

Speed

Speed does not just consist of total body speed, but is made up of a player's reaction time to a stimulus, his ability to make short bursts of speed and his ability to sustain fast body movement. The essential variables will be factors such as acceleration (i.e. body and/or limb speed), the production of force and anticipation. A soccer player will rarely run the same distances as an athletic sprinter, covering 10–20 or 30–60 metres (11–22 or 33–66 yards) at the most. In athletic events retardation (slowing down) will occur at around 60 metres (66 yards), with the best sprinters being those who hold 'form' best. However, form is not so prevalent in soccer as sprinting may well involve having a ball at your feet, or consist of evasive, angled running. What is required is the ability to produce (frequently) rapid bursts of short sprint speed coupled with an ability to react quickly to a stimulus, for example an opponent breaking into space on a blind-side run who needs rapid covering.

In soccer training, developing anticipatory skills is vital to speed work, especially speed of mental response. Protracted repetitions of carefully selected soccer drills in small-sided situations may well have a sound educational effect in decreasing reaction time in matches. This is what gives an individual the 'edge' which is so vital, especially to players who rely on speed like the striker or the goalkeeper.

Of course speed is to some extent hereditary, such that improvements made in training will be relatively small. Thus good runners in soccer will need to have powerful leg muscles and not be too heavy in the upper body, as acceleration is proportional to the weight of the player (mass) and the propulsion applied (the force exerted by the lower limbs when they are in contact with the ground). Speed is also dependent on the development of other physical components such as strength and flexibility. For example all players need to kick the ball for distance and accuracy (of pass/shot) many times in a game. Limb speed is vital and a muscle group's power and range of movement potential is the key factor. Therefore, for short anaerobic speed work and speed endurance, leg strength is crucial to the footballer.

The key factor to remember in training is to concentrate on developing stride length and frequency.

Power

If speed equals distance over time, then power is the product of force multiplied by speed. Field tests such as vertical jumps and standing broad jumps are simple measures of athletic power. These tests make it possible to calculate work output by comparing the positive work done (e.g. moving against the resistance of an opposing force in a vertical jump) to that which is wasted. The footballer has to cope with a great variety of sub-maximal work demands. Some players will have to demonstrate explosive movement potential, especially goalkeepers, strikers and defenders when they have to leap to catch, head or chest control high balls. Good boots should provide grip (traction) and maximise force production when the player makes contact with the ground.

Flexibility

Flexibility is an aspect of physical fitness which is invariably overlooked or underemphasised by soccer players and coaches. Medical research shows that lack of flexibility is not uncommon in men. Soccer players seem to be more overtly concerned with ball skills and tactical awareness, and continue to neglect the development of flexibility. Perhaps this is because coaches rationalise what they do in terms of the pressures to succeed, and consider skills and

strategies more essential in their player preparation. However, it may also be the case that coaches and players of all abilities have never really been taught the positive benefits of flexibility routines.

Flexibility is concerned with the range of movement that the human body is capable of, particularly that movement which occurs at joint complexes such as the ankle, the knee, the hip and the shoulder joint. Flexibility training should increase the pliability of ligaments. Thus hip flexor stretch exercises will increase hip mobility, which is essential in sprint work. Increased mobility helps to minimise hamstring injury, which is a common ailment of soccer players.

It is dangerous to generalise too much about flexibility; what must happen is that the player and his coach together assess the nature of the physical work demands. Initially, a general programme of flexibility exercises is advisable, becoming gradually sport-specific and a regular part of the daily/weekly training regime. In soccer, it is imperative to develop routines which aid hip mobility and promote great knee joint stability. If these routines then become a regular feature of the overall training programme, they *will* produce improvements in mobility and stability, and may well have a positive effect on strength and speed.

Strength

Strength may be defined as the ability to exert maximum force from a single muscular contraction. In soccer, players have to be strong so that they can exert force during moments of body contact/collision and general running (speed and speed endurance work), and when executing isolated skills such as kicking and throwing. There will be few moments in a game when a player has to exert maximum force and rely on pure strength alone, but having good, all round strength will be beneficial to soccer performance. For example, having a well-developed musculature will prevent the injuries that often result from lower limb contact and collision. Medical research has shown that leg strength is vital for soccer players and that professional players who engaged in a strength training programme for a year (as a supplement to their general conditioning) showed significant increases in concentric and eccentric leg strength and kicking performance. Also, given that the modern game increasingly uses strategies such as the throw-in as an attacking set-piece ploy, upper-body strength and flexibility are vital in the production of a long throw. Previously, this type of strength specificity was only considered important to the goalkeeper, but now it is recognised as necessary to outfield players as well.

Body composition

The overall physique of a player, his body shape and size, has a bearing on his performance and/or the playing role he takes on. Researchers in sports medicine often refer to these factors in terms of body composition.

People can be classified according to their body shape (somatotyping), with individuals being divided into the categories of endomorphy, mesomorphy and ectomorphy. Research indicates that mesomorphy is the dominant somatotype in footballers. Clearly, goalkeepers, strikers and central defenders need to have a real physical presence in terms of height and body size. Midfield players tend to be the smallest members of a team in terms of physical stature and the lightest (the average weight is 70 kg (11 st.)). This may be because soccer is a game that requires continuous bouts of effort at a reasonably high intensity for long periods, such that large amounts of physical bulk are a disadvantage. Sports medicine research has shown that footballers tend to be quite lean, with low percentage body-fat scores. Although hereditary factors mean that individuals are only able to change their body shape marginally, the statistics show that regular training can alter body composition, that is lean body-weight and body-fat scores.

Female soccer players

Very little research has been conducted on female soccer players, possibly due to the fact that it is a 'new' sport in terms of organisation and participation. Women's soccer is increasingly popular in Britain (especially England) and Australia. Recently, at international level, these two countries have produced the following information about their international players, via laboratory testing.

	England	Australia
Average age	25.3 yrs	24.4 yrs
Average height	165.7 cm	158.1 cm
	(5ft 5in)	(5ft 2in)
Average weight	59.0 kg	55.4 kg
	(130 lb)	(122 lb)
Average % body fat	21.2%	20.8%
Average $\dot{V}O_2$max	51.97	47.9

FITNESS TRAINING

Introduction

As we saw in the previous chapter the main components of fitness for soccer players are endurance, strength, speed, flexibility and power. The soccer player will have to invest considerable time and effort to see a significant 'return' for his efforts, that is an improvement in performance. A truly professional approach to physical conditioning has still to materialise at professional club level, due to a lack of facilities and coaches with suitable in-depth knowledge of fitness and the principles of training. Also, throughout the game there is a more overt concern for the development of individual ball skills or team strategies. But it has to be remembered that when fitness deteriorates in training and in match play, these individual skills and team strategies also suffer. There is a feeling that fitness should be primarily the concern of the individual and not the coach, but all too often in team games an individual will play to get fit rather than get fit to play.

Principles of training

Specificity

Specificity relates to the need to know which energy system(s) are utilised during performance and which physical actions predominate. The coach may start by monitoring what a player does in a game, tracking him with a video over a number of games, or performing simple pen and paper analysis in order to determine the specific demands placed upon the player. A time and motion analysis (i.e. work to rest ratio) or a technical involvement analysis may give a clearer, more objective picture.

Specificity also relates to the level of involvement of an individual in modes of training. Thus while weight-training will improve strength, it may well limit flexibility, and any work done will show gains that are specific to a particular muscle group or joint complex. It generally helps if we remember that training should simulate as closely as possible what happens in actual games, and that training effects are closely linked to the nature of the training undertaken.

Overload

To attain a suitable level of fitness, you have to work physically hard. If you are a club player who aspires to international level then you will have to work harder, and place yourself in regular, stressful training regimes that overload the body to produce the physiological/biological changes necessary in order to cope with the higher physical performance demands. Three key variables that need to be mentioned in relation to the overload principle are as follows:

F – frequency of training
I – intensity of training
T – (time) duration of training.

Frequency refers simply to the number of fitness (not skills) sessions per day, week, month and year. Research has shown that training at least three times a week will ensure improvements in physical performance.

The intensity of training refers to the physical loading that is structured in any single session or series of sessions. Clearly each soccer player will have a different physical work capacity when starting a structured programme. To what extent the player improves overall, or in particular components of physical fitness, will be dependent upon his initial capacity and the extent to which he is continually overloaded. If a player is not placed under physical stress during his fitness training sessions he will not improve his fitness, but will merely maintain his existing level of fitness; in this situation we say that the level of intensity is constant. However, if he is asked to work at a greater intensity (e.g. performing a familiar sprint set with a decreased recovery period) and eventually comes to cope with this extra work demand, perhaps after a period of extreme physical stress or discomfort, then a training effect occurs. Coaches should exercise caution when setting the level of intensity of any programme, and make sure that the intensity only increases gradually.

Fitness is not a static phenomenon, but is subject to change, so we must remember that absolute intensity of exercise is relative to current fitness. A player's body will change and adapt to the stresses placed on it, such that the sessions that seemed hard initially will appear normal after a period of time. Comparing your heart-rate before and after exercise (see below) is a good way of determining the intensity of training and your ability to cope. Furthermore, keeping a record in a training diary of statistics such as heart-rates, training distances and loads, and the nature of training is extremely valuable, since it enables you to monitor progress over time and to evaluate which particular training programmes work best for you. The frequency of overload in training often depends upon a combination of the intensity and the duration of training. Duration relates to the specific amount of time spent involved in fitness work; for example the fitness 'work-out' may be done in isolation or as part of an overall session where it is just one of many aspects of training.

Monitoring the pulse by means of the radial artery (wrist) and the carotid artery (neck)

However, training must be of sufficient duration to allow a training effect to occur.

Motivation and discipline

Determining how often a player should train and measuring rates of progress is relatively simple, but anticipating how he will respond psychologically to a training regime is more difficult. Thus the human factor, or psychological variable, in the design and execution of training programmes, is crucial. The player must realise that training involves a commitment to long hours of work over many months and years. Some players have a temperament which means that they are intrinsically motivated to train and play. However, not all players have high levels of concentration and application, and often individuals experience a loss of interest or boredom when training for any length of time.

Discipline is thus an important factor in training, both in the sense of a discipline which is imposed on the player by means of a schedule and in terms of an 'inner-discipline' represented in his response to training. A coach can help by introducing variety to the training programme, especially in terms of the nature, quality and quantity of work done. This mixture will do much to foster enjoyment and a keen anticipation of training. The coach may try disguising physical training occasionally, for example by using game-related duels (i.e. small-sided games) which involve pressure and which benefit players and coach alike.

Reversibility

If players do become bored with physical training and drop out of this aspect of preparation, then in time their fitness levels will deteriorate. Injury, illness and inactivity during the off season are all common occurrences which will lead to a partial or total loss of physical fitness. Peak physical fitness is very hard to attain but easy to lose. There is no permanency to fitness. It is important, therefore, to promote a positive concern for daily, lifelong fitness and, when in competition, to minimise the length of time spent away from any training regime.

Planning the training programme

A training programme for any sport has to be built around the specific competitions or competition phases that occur in any year (see figs 116 and 117).

To give appropriate consideration to the physiological, technical and psychological aspects of soccer performance, a soccer coach or management team ought to plan in a cyclical way. Within this yearly cycle, especially for conditioning purposes, the player, coach and management team might collectively target training cycles of 2–8 weeks' duration (a mesocycle), or a 7-day cycle between Saturday matches (a microcycle). The variables which might govern the planning include:

- the season's starting and finishing dates
- league matches against the most feared opponents
- cup competition dates
- official rest/holiday period
- established periods for technical (skills) and strategical development
- established periods for any 'maintenance' of fitness.

Off season period

Ideally, this period should involve a spell of rest and recuperation coupled with bouts of active recovery from the physical and psychological intensity of the previous season's soccer. Unfortunately, many players of all levels of ability regard the off season as a time of inactivity. Post-competition there *should* be a tapering away of training intensity but *not* a total withdrawal. The important thing is to provide a mental release from the pressures of competition, which is catered for through the use of light-hearted, fun sessions, while at the same time maintaining a sound platform of fitness ready for the new season.

Pre-season period

This period marks the beginning of a highly organised, structured cycle (ideally 8 weeks prior to competition). The main objective of this period is to reach the fitness levels that soccer is known to demand. Some fitness advisers suggest training and preparing for the worst possible scenario, or engaging in 'supra'

Fig. 116   A yearly cycle
of involvement in soccer

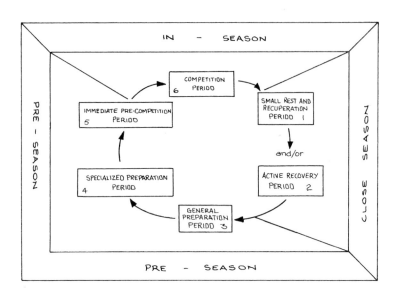

Fig. 117   A chronological breakdown of a yearly soccer programme

July	August	Sept	Oct	Nov	Dec	Jan	Feb	March	April	May	June

Pre-season	In-season							Close season			

Preparation Period	League and Cup Competition Period	Rest and Active Recovery Period

(beyond known maximum) match fitness work, which are good ideas both physiologically and psychologically. This is also the time when, logically, the player should begin to do highly specialised training.

Competition period

Traditionally, during the soccer season the emphasis is placed upon individual skill development and strategical/tactical manoeuvres. Time devoted to conditioning decreases proportionally as the time given to executing set-piece practices increases. However, too many soccer players do not find time – and the time *is* available even during the season – to do conditioning work. Small improvements in physical performance are still possible, especially if the sessions concentrate on quality work. The least the player should expect of himself is that he maintains the level of fitness he worked so hard to achieve in the off and pre-season

periods, so that he retains the 'edge' over any opponent.

The coach can help, even in those sessions which concentrate on drills and set-piece practices, by planning well and minimising the time wasted. Unit work can still be made intensely physically demanding through imaginative coaching. Players are rightly reluctant to spend time unproductively during in-season training, which places the onus on the coach to structure sessions carefully. The coach ought to share the tasks of planning, decision-making and goal-setting with his players, especially the senior players in his squad. Players will respond far better when they know the objectives and desired outcome of practices.

The following is a detailed outline of the structure and function of a year-round programme of soccer training.

Cycle 1: off season

Period 1: short rest and recuperation period. Duration: 2 weeks.

Aim: physical and psychological release from the tension of competition.

Content: 1 individual or team holiday
2 low intensity jogging 2/3 times per week (30+ mins)
3 engaging in another sport(s), e.g. golf or swimming.

Period 2: active recovery period. Duration: 2–4 weeks.

Aims: 1 maintaining aerobic physical activity
2 concentrating initially on components of physical fitness not usually given great attention during the season, i.e. strength, power, flexibility
3 encouraging self-monitoring, i.e. start fitness diaries and diet/weight recording.

Content: 1 begin Fartlek, i.e. varied, sub-maximal running on interesting terrain/environment, e.g. running with a partner(s)
2 start weight-training (free weights or multi-station) for strength or muscular endurance and power, especially for the large muscle groups, e.g. half-squat, or bench press and clean.
3 begin a general flexibility routine
4 do ball juggling skills on your own.

N.B. Fartlek work and weight-training can run concurrently (back-to-back) on the same training day for 3 weeks. Thus a run on Monday, Wednesday and Friday would be followed by weight-training.

Cycle 2: pre-season

Period 3: general preparation period. Duration: 4+ weeks.

Aims: 1 to further build on the work done in period 2, the active recovery period.
2 to continue to encourage the self-monitoring work done by players and to reinforce the value of this work by bringing the squad together occasionally for discussions with fitness experts/consultants, who should be linked to the club.

Content: 1 Fartlek runs in groups over varied terrain. Ask players to 'lead' sections of the run and provide training routines within the Fartlek. Record the times attained.
2 weight-training. Where possible move from muscular endurance work (i.e. many repetitions with low weights) to strength work (small sets and repetitions with heavier weights). Record the weights lifted
3 Specialised flexibility exercises done in preparation for the sprint work to follow in period 4, i.e. concentrate on flexibility drills linked to increasing the range of motion in the lower body
4 conduct 2 time-trials over 5,000 m during the middle and the end of this period, to get a base indicator of aerobic capacity
5 conduct a multi-stage fitness test (continuous shuttle run) at the end of this period, or any other specific fitness test deemed appropriate by a sports scientist.

Period 4: specialist preparation period. Duration: 4+ weeks.

Aims: 1 to reach the high levels of fitness required for competition, concentrating especially on anaerobic training/speed work
2 to tailor individualised programmes of training from information gained previously. Monitoring and evaluation are essential here
3 to begin highly specialised individual and unit skills practices, and to evaluate the past season's practices and performances.

Content: 1 complete 2 distance courses per week (i.e. 3–4 miles at a 7-minute-mile pace) for the first 2 weeks
2 introduce interval running (1 set) in each of the first 2 weeks
3 conduct 1 highly specialised weights session on a day when you do *not* do interval training or speed work

4 begin high quality, coach-led skills sessions of 1½ hours' duration to develop motivated and slick ball-work sessions
5 watch videos, and build team strategies
6 continue with specialist flexibility work (this is especially important before any sharper speed/interval work)
7 try introducing plyometric exercises for 1 session per week.

Period 5: immediate pre-competition period. Duration: 2 weeks.
Aims: **1** to bring players to a peak ready for the new season
2 to assess objectively the players' fitness and to evaluate the training regime, especially from period 3 onwards (i.e. an 8–10-week block of work)
3 to engage in pre-season matches to test fitness and tactics.
Content: **1** to continue the interval work and develop speed; players will need 2 speed sessions to bring them to their peak. Do not forget to do some speed endurance work, and introduce plyometric exercises for those players who can cope with the work
2 maintain at least 1 aerobic steady-state run of 30+ minutes per week
3 conduct 1 or 2 weight-training sessions which are 'maintenance' orientated, i.e. they retain the strength accumulated over the last 8–10 weeks
4 continue flexibility work (N.B. Block the weight-training and flexibility sessions together and do sprint work at convenient times in your club skills sessions)
5 engage a specialist team of sports scientists and choose a day on which to hold highly specific testing which monitors improvement.

Cycle 3: Competition
Period 6: competition period. Duration: 30+ weeks.
Aim: To retain a concern for every aspect of fitness, that is motor fitness, psychological fitness and physiological fitness, that contributes to a winning formula.
Content: **1** continue with aerobic running, especially in the form of active recovery runs the day after mid-week and Saturday matches
2 continue with weight-training for strength, using 1 or possibly 2 specialist maintenance sessions so as not to experience reversals in strength or power
3 concentrate and even extend anaerobic running work, i.e. interval training, to 1 session per week
4 concentrate on sprinting, i.e. speed and speed endurance work for 2 sessions per week
5 conduct a circuit (indoor) session once a week to improve muscular endurance
6 aim for quality both in terms of skill execution and fitness work in any skills session
7 conduct structured testing sessions and study the information contained in players' training diaries. Also, check players' nutritional intake weekly.

Aerobic endurance training methods

The following exercises should form the basis of any soccer player's aerobic training, upon which he can then build other fitness components.

Continuous running

This involves the soccer player running in his free time. The greater the frequency and the duration of these runs in terms of time and distance, the better. Progression is the key, with the player gradually increasing the demands on himself and setting himself a series of targets, e.g. 4 miles in 30 minutes, then 4 miles in 28 minutes (a 30-second decrease per mile). Jogging is a good physical exercise for soccer players to start with, and will have a number of positive effects.

1. The lungs function more efficiently (more air reaches the blood as it circulates through the

lungs), resulting in an improved $\dot{V}O_2$ max. (i.e. the capacity of the player's aerobic system).
2. The transport of oxygen by the blood to the muscles is increased.
3. The heart becomes a more efficient pump with an improved work capacity.
4. Both the resting and the active pulse rates can drop, indicating improved cardio-vascular fitness.
5. There is better utilisation of the blood vessels and an increased creation of small blood vessels in the working muscles, which is a sign of a better circulatory system.

In order to make running enjoyable, try running with a team-mate so that you can motivate each other. Devise a variety of routes which are aesthetically pleasing and physically challenging. Research suggests that you should run for at least 25–30 minutes 3 times per week. (A good, fit soccer player ought to aim to do 4–5 miles 3 times per week at a 6–7-minute mile pace.) In order to monitor the intensity of your run, take your pulse at the mid-point and again at the end of your run (either by hand or by using a commercial heart-rate tester, which can be worn like a wrist watch). The norm is about 120–160 beats per minute for a 4–5-mile jog.

Speed play or Fartlek running

If you are searching for variety in your endurance running, then try Fartlek running. (Fartlek is the Swedish for speed play and is used by many famous athletes.) Fartlek today is more than just a change in the form of training; it has become a type of informal interval training, and is ideal for soccer as it develops both aerobic and anaerobic capacities. Working on a variety of surfaces (e.g. grass, sand or tarmac), inclines and environments (e.g. forests, sand-dunes, open countryside) allows the soccer player to adapt the work and rest intervals according to his needs. This is not to say the training lacks structure because contained within any session are a series of alternating fast and slow runs.

Session 1
1. Jog steadily for 5–8 minutes.
2. Do 5 minutes' calisthenics/stretching in an open space.
3. Run at a fast, steady pace for 5 minutes.
4. Walk briskly for 3 minutes.
5. Run at a fast, steady pace for 8 minutes.
6. Walk briskly for 5 minutes.

Training principle key variables	Aerobic running steady state work Training dose	Anaerobic running sprint work Training dose
Intensity	Heart-rate at 85% of max.	Heart-rate at 180 beats per min. +
Frequency	3–5 times per week (1 session per day)	3 times per week (1 session per day)
Duration	12+ weekly block	8+ weekly block
	Distance covered in a single session – 4 to 5 miles	Distance covered in a single session – 2 miles

Fig. 118   A running schedule for a soccer player (adapted from Fox, E. and Mathews, D., The Physiological Basis of Physical Education and Athletics, 3rd edition, Saunders Publishing, New York, 1981)

7. Jog for 2 minutes.
8. A cycle of 6×200 metres (50 metres jog, 50 metres stride, 50 metres sprint, 50 metres walk recovery).
9. Jog for 5 minutes with 1 hill run of 30+ metres every minute.
10. Jog for 2–3 minutes, with repeated calisthenics/stretching as a warm-down.

Session 2
1. Jog as a warm-up for 5 minutes.
2. Do stretching work with a partner for 5 minutes.
3. Run $\frac{1}{2}$–$\frac{3}{4}$ mile at a fast, steady pace.
4. Walk briskly for 3–5 minutes.
5. Stride downhill (on a gentle slope) for technique. Alternate this with a short walk, then sprint back up the same slope until fatigued. Do this for 5–8 minutes.
6. Jog at an easy pace for 5 minutes.
7. Jog with 50 metres sprinting for every 200 metres approximately (alternately led sprints).
8. Run continually increasing the pace for 3 minutes.
9. Finish with a run at fast pace for 1 minute.
10. Jog and do stretching exercises as a warm-down.

What Fartlek training does, with its intermittent bouts of fast running and steady-state jogging, is to produce periods in the work-out when the body is pushed into an anaerobic situation and has to cope with oxygen debt. The overall effect is to promote quicker recovery rates from strenuous exercise. What happens on the Fartlek run is exactly what should happen in the game, that is that players make many quality fast runs with only a limited active recovery time. In both training and in matches, it is important to make the most of rest periods.

Interval running

This involves performing a set number of runs over a specified distance with structured periods of recovery or rest. It is a very strenuous type of activity but one which is immensely profitable in its application to soccer. Usually, it is advisable to carry out this type of training after a sound base of cardio-respiratory fitness has already been built up. Interval training is beneficial to both aerobic and anaerobic energy systems and will therefore help delay fatigue. By doing interval work involving lengthy exercise with multiple repetitions and active recovery periods, great stress is placed on the oxygen transport system. Consequently the aerobic energy system is developed as the working muscles improve their oxidative capacity. Improvements will occur in heart and lung functioning as a result of a protracted period of interval work.

3. Nature of the interval work: the pace of the runs, which is dictated by time or the prescribed intensity of effort (e.g. 80% max speed for 50 metres).
4. Repetitions: the number of 'bouts' of exercise within one set (e.g. 6 × 200 metres).

The key factors to remember with interval work are as follows.
1. Longer work intervals means more endurance is being taxed.
2. It is very useful as an out-of-season preparatory aerobic training regime.
3. Intensity of effort will vary depending on the need to stress aerobic or anaerobic systems.
4. The closer to maximum sprint speed the player trains, the fewer repetitions he need do.
5. Rest intervals should be structured so that repeat runs of the same intensity are possible.
6. Active rest (a slow jog or positive walk) allows for the dispersal of lactic acid and thus generates better possibilities for recovery and further work.

A typical 'prescription' for interval training might be:

1. A 5-minute jog
2. flexibility work

Interval work	Repetitions	Training distance	Training time	Recovery
3. Set 1	6 repetitions	200 m	35 secs	with 1.25 mins jog back
4. Set 2	6 repetitions	100 m	15 secs	with 0.45 mins jog back

The following variables need to be carefully considered when constructing interval running programmes.

1. Work interval: the overall length of time of physical exercise.
2. Rest/recovery interval: the length of time of the rest period between individual repetitions and between sets of repetitions.

Sports scientists suggest recording player's optimal running times for distances of 50 metres, 100 metres, 200 metres and 1,500 metres. With training distances up to 200 metres they then simply add an incremental time to the optimal time (see table below).

Distance (m)	Optimum time (secs)	Increment	Interval time (sec)/work rate
50	6·0	+1	7·0
100	12·5	+3	15·5
200	28·0	+5	33·0

For interval training distances of 400 metres, the coach looks at the player's 1,600 metres time, divides it by 4 to get a base time and knocks between 1 and 4 seconds off to get a reasonable 400 m interval training work-rate. Thus a player who has a 1,600 metre time of 6 minutes would have a 400 metre interval work-rate of 1 minute and 26 seconds. For interval training work of 800–1600 metres simply *add* 4 seconds to each lap, relative to the slips in your 1,600 m best time. In this case a player whose 1,600 metre time is 7 minutes is deemed to have an average 400 metre time of 1 minute and 45 seconds, an 800 metre interval work-rate of 3 minutes and 38 seconds (+8 seconds) and a 1,600 metre interval work-rate of 7 minutes and 16 seconds (+16 seconds).

Finally, important consideration must be given to the number of repetitions and, therefore, the total distance the player is expected to run, and to the duration and type of recovery involved. Generally speaking, most interval sessions cover between 1,750 metres and 2,500 metres in order to generate improvement in the energy systems. The work to rest/relief ratio is usually dependent upon the distance and the intensity of running, as shown in the following table.

Session 2
The same warm-up procedure is followed as in Session 1.
Set 1 6×200 metres at a pace of 30 secs with 90 sec. relief.
Set 2 4×100 metres at a pace of 15 secs with 45 sec. relief.
Set 3 4×50 metres at a pace of 6 secs with 18 sec. relief.
Warm-down as before.

Session 3
Warm-up as in the previous sessions.
Set 1 3×800 metres at a pace of 3 mins 30 secs with 4 min 45 sec. relief.
Set 2 2×300 metres at a pace of 1 min. with 3 min relief.
Warm-down as before.

Recovery *between* sets is vital. Researchers suggest that the heart-rate (monitored by a pulse count) should be down to approximately 120 beats per minute before another interval set is started. This might mean 3–5 minutes' slow jogging in between sets with periodic pulse monitoring by players and coach. Also, the nature of the recovery between sets might be jogging (active relief) or it might simply consist

Distance (m)	Interval time/work-rate (sec)	Rest/relief ratio	Total activity cycle (1 rep.)
50 m	7·0	1:3 (21 secs)	28 secs
100 m	15·5	1:3 (46·5 secs)	62 secs
200 m	33·0	1:3 (1 min. 39 secs)	2 min. 12 secs
400 m	1 min. 30 secs	1:2 (3 mins)	4 mins 30 secs
800 m	3 mins 30 secs	1:1·5 (4 mins 45 secs)	8 mins 15 secs

Pre-season and in-season interval training routines

Session 1

Warm-up	jog
	stretching (general)
	jog
	stretching (specific)

Set 1 8×50 metres at a pace of 0.7 secs with 20 sec. relief.
Set 2 6×100 metres at a pace of 15.5 secs with 45 sec. relief.
Set 3 4×150 metres at a pace of 24.0 secs with 75 sec. relief.
Set 4 2×200 metres at a pace of 33.0 secs with 90 sec. relief.
Warm-down: jog and stretching.

of kinetic flexibility work or plain walking (rest relief). Interval training is valuable not only because it replicates the demands of a soccer game, but also because it allows the coach to systematically monitor and evaluate a player's progress (by recording times), which requires little sophisticated equipment other than a good stopwatch.

Muscular endurance training methods

Soccer is a game which needs high levels of muscular endurance. Sprinting forwards and backwards at speed, lateral running, leaping to head or catch a ball, diving, driving into front block tackles, sliding into tackles, twisting and turning are all performed repeatedly within one activity cycle. Add to that the fact that body contact and collisions are commonplace, and that much of the work is done at speed, and the need for muscular endurance becomes clear. Without question, the most common, simple and effective type of training to improve muscular endurance is circuit training.

Through engaging in a general fitness circuit 3 times per week over 6 weeks' duration, significant improvements in overall fitness, muscular strength, speed and, possibly, flexibility are likely to occur. Circuit training involves using your own body-weight as resistance, and variety can be introduced by using a simple apparatus that enables the player to train at home, outside, or in a small gymnasium. Usually, any one 'circuit' consists of between 6 and 15 exercise stations, with work at each station lasting for 1 minute. A 30-second rest is taken after each station before moving around the stations in a circular fashion. Clearly, the best circuit for a soccer player is one that is soccer-specific, has stations that mimic game action and/or puts those muscle groups that would be exerted repeatedly in a match under stress. Thus, to seek a particular physiological effect (e.g. developing muscular endurance in the lower limbs and thereby making overall muscular strength gains) it is necessary to structure a particular type of circuit.

It is important when designing circuits to look for a balanced loading which alternates the demands on muscular groups. For example, in a 12-station circuit a coach might concentrate on:

station 1: upper trunk
station 2: lower trunk } repeated 4 times.
station 3: lower limbs

A 12-station soccer-specific circuit may work on a cycle which overloads the lower limbs as in the following example:

station 1: upper trunk
            (chest, arms,
            upper back)
station 2: lower limbs (legs)   } repeated
station 3: lower trunk   } 3 times
            (stomach, hips,
            lower back)
station 4: lower limbs (legs)

In this way, no one muscle group is repeatedly over-taxed, which means local muscular recovery can take place, and overall the body's main

organs and circulatory system are being increasingly stressed.

Another important factor concerning the use of circuit training is that it does not take up too much time. For example, a 15-station cycle with 1 minute of work and 30 seconds' rest would only require $22\frac{1}{2}$ minutes' activity time plus the warm-up and warm-down. The following are some other possible circuit designs.

1. Identify 10 exercise stations. Work flat out for 1 minute with a partner scoring each repetition. Record the maximum for each station and allow 1 minute for recovery. Aim for 75% of the maximum score on each repetition, and repeat the circuit 3 times (with 30 second rest intervals, and 3 minutes between each circuit).
2. Identify 10 exercise stations, 1 being a shuttle run between 2 set points. This run should last between 45 seconds and 1 minute. The work interval is governed by the speed of the players on the shuttle station.
3. Identify 10 exercise stations. Construct 3 targets on a sliding scale of difficulty (i.e. the number of reps) for each station. For example, with a press-up station using a 30 second work interval the 'easy' target would be 5 reps, the 'moderate' target would be 12 reps and the 'hard' target would be 20 reps.
4. Design a continuous movement circuit, much like an assault course, with a mixture of running and clearing obstacles by jumping, hopping, making forward rolls, etc. The players perform circuits in groups over a set time (e.g. 2 mins), then they change and let another group take over. It is excellent motivation for players to record the number of circuits completed in the time (e.g. $2\frac{3}{4}$ circuits).

The result of this type of training seems most likely to be gains in muscular endurance and strength, which suggests that this work would form an ideal part of an out-of-season conditioning programme, especially as it is economical in terms of the work period and the setting-up time.

Soccer-specific circuit

This circuit seeks to build up local muscular endurance in the lower limbs especially, to improve overall muscular strength and to have a slight positive effect on the cardio-vascular system.

Station	Exercise
1	prone medicine ball throw
2	astride jumps (with the arms behind the back or holding a weight to the chest)
3	alternate single leg raises using a wall bar (with the knees bent)
4	continuous shuttle runs between 2 points
5	press-ups
6	step-ups
7	alternate leg lunges
8	continuous shuttle runs between 4 points of a diamond shape
9	double-leg throw aways
10	run and jump to head a target (e.g. 2 suspended footballs 5 metres apart)
11	hyperextensions
12	continuous shuttle run (same as number 8 but alternate backward and forward running)

Thus it is clear that soccer players need to do plenty of work in order to train the physical component of endurance. Continuous, steady-state running, Fartlek work, interval training and circuit training are all well proven methods which can raise levels of aerobic and local muscular endurance. This component of fitness needs to be developed in the off and pre-season periods and maintained during the season by means of a planned personal fitness regime.

Strength training

This is an area of training about which many players and coaches are still lacking in knowledge. As a result, myths and general disinformation abound as to the value of strength training for soccer. However, strength is without question the foundation stone to soccer fitness. It is a physical fitness component which can dictate a player's speed, muscular endurance capacity and power output and it is clear when we consider the nature of the action in soccer that players need high levels of these qualities. Leading clubs have now recognised this and know that they must include strength training work as part of their overall conditioning.

Basically, strength training should consist of a series of resistance exercises in which the body's muscle groups work against an immovable or a movable object. To be more precise, strength conditioning can involve working against a number of different forms of resistance, thus producing a variety of methods for training (see the table below).

The soccer player should subject particular muscle groups to stress so that a positive adaptation can occur. This means that the fibres in the working muscles will increase in size, so producing extra muscle mass (known as hypertrophy). The soccer player will *not* need excessive muscle hypertrophy, but he will need good general strength and especially leg strength for explosive activity (e.g. sprinting, jumping and diving). The most sensible type of strength training for the soccer player is a programme which starts off using the multi-station machines and progresses to using free weights for very specific exercises.

Another idea might be to combine these methods with your own body resistance exercises. Simple exercises like push-ups and abdominal curls are excellent, because they can be done by a whole group in a small area, with players co-operating or competing against one another. Clearly, the key in strength training is

Resistance	Exercise in training	Type of muscular contraction
Constant	Static: applying force against an immovable object such as a door frame.	Isometric
Variable	Dynamic: applying force while the resistance load changes, using a multi-gym and free weights.	Isotonic
Accommodating	Dynamic: applying force to the cybex machine which governs the velocity of contraction.	Isokinetic

specificity, and after the player comes to know his own physical limitations an individualised programme can be constructed.

The following strength training programme is recommended for soccer players because it takes account of the demands of the game. However, you may find it difficult to get access to the range of equipment that is necessary.

Individual strength training programme (Multi-station exercises)

Leg Press

1. Sit with your feet squarely on the foot rests.
2. Make sure the buttocks are in such a position that there is an angle of 90° between the upper and the lower legs before pushing the legs forwards into a straight leg position.
3. Slowly return to the starting position and repeat.

This exercise strengthens the legs and the buttocks.

Bench press

1. Lie on your back with your feet flat on the floor and the knees bent at 90°. Make sure that you do *not* arch your lower back when pressing the weight up.
2. Press upwards to full arm extension (breathing out as you work).

This exercise strengthens the arms, the chest and the shoulders.

Leg extension

1. Sit upright with your feet tucked under the roll pads, and the knees at 90°.
2. Holding the side or underneath of the seat, drive upwards with the lower legs and the feet, exhaling as you lift the weight up horizontal to the leg position.

This exercise strengthens the thigh muscles.

Leg flexion

1. Lie on your front with your heels tucked under the roll pad.

2. Holding the end or sides of the bench, raise your heels towards your buttocks until your lower leg is at or just beyond an inverse 90°
3. Breathe out as you lift, then take the weight slowly back down.

This exercise strengthens the backs of the leg muscles.

Free weights

Military press
1. Rest the bar on your upper chest, with your feet shoulder width apart.
2. Hold the bar slightly wider than shoulder width with an overgrasp grip, keeping the elbows well under the bar.
3. Press the bar to full arm extension above your head (breathing out as you lift).

This exercise strengthens the shoulders and the arms.

Half-squat

1. Rest the bar on your neck and shoulders, with your feet approximately shoulder width apart.
2. Hold the bar with your hands wide of your shoulders.
3. On commencing, drop your body down until your thighs are just parallel to the floor, keeping your back straight and your head up.
4. Drive up out of this position, forcing your hips upwards and slightly forwards (exhaling as you move upwards).

This exercise strengthens the legs and the lower back.

Power clean

1. Address the bar, standing with your feet nearly shoulder width apart.
2. Place your feet under the bar and use an overgrasp grip which is slightly wider than shoulder width.
3. To start the lift adopt a crouching position with your knees inside your elbows, your back flat and your head up.
4. Next, drive explosively with your legs and your hips until your legs are straight.
5. Follow this with a drive from your feet

(rising on to your toes) and a pull with your arms.

6.   When maximum upward extension occurs, move your elbows downwards rapidly to bring your arms under the bar and so support the weight on your chest.

7.   At all times keep the bar close to your body (i.e. the legs, the stomach and the chest) when lifting upwards.

This exercise strengthens many body parts, especially the ankles, the knees, the hips, the back, the arms and the shoulders.

General guidelines when working with weights

1.   Seek expert advice before embarking on a strength training schedule.

2.   Follow a structured programme which is written down and evaluated by means of a 'reflective' monitoring of the weight lifted relative to each exercise (i.e. it doesn't ask too much of you).

3.   Always lift with a training partner, especially when working with free weights. *Never* be afraid to ask for support when lifting, particularly with the heavy weights.

4.   Start lifting as soon as the off season begins, and look to build all-round strength (i.e. devise a general schedule which uses body resistance and multi-station exercises involving high repetitions and a gradual weight increase).

5.   Only begin to specialise after a period of preparation in the off season. Use the pyramid system of training during this specialist phase. Engage in 3 sessions per week during any specialist strength training regime.

6.   Once the playing season arrives then seek to 'maintain' strength by performing 1 or 2 sessions weekly. Look to fit these sessions around playing and technical training.

Guidelines for designing strength training routines

1.   Any form of weight-training attempts to overload the working muscle. Low resistances (light weights) and high (multiple) repetitions will develop muscular endurance. High resistances (heavy weights) and low (minimal) repetitions will develop muscular strength.

2.   A repetition is the complete lift from start through lift to recovery.

3.   A maximum repetition is that number of

repetitions which can be performed with a given load without stopping. Identifying the maximum weight lifted over 10 repetitions (10–RM) is the key to the progressive resistance weight-training which builds strength. A typical progressive resistance 'set' might be structured as follows:

> **set 1**: 10 reps on   50% of 10=RM
> **set 2**: 10 reps on   75% of 10=RM
> **set 3**: 10 reps on 100% of 10=RM.

When you can perform between 12–15 reps on any third set then a new 10-RM has to be calculated (i.e. progression will have to occur as strength grows).

4.   Another type of schedule uses the 'pyramid' method. Here you need to identify the maximum load that can be lifted twice (2–RM), and then design a schedule with progressive resistance and decreasing repetitions. Thus if a maximum 2 – RM bench press weight was 100 kg (220 lb) then the schedule might be:

> 10 reps at   40 kg (88 lb)
> 8 reps at   60 kg (132 lb)
> 4 reps at   80 kg (176 lb)
> 2 reps at 100 kg (220 lb).

5.   A set constitutes the number of specified repetitions in any one lifting routine, for example for the bench press exercise 5 sets consist of 10 reps on 100 kg (220 lb).

6.   Always lift any weight with *control*. Excessive speed of movement will make the exercise brief and will minimise the opportunities to build strength.

7.   Never attempt to lift a weight that you think is too heavy.

8.   Always breathe regularly throughout the lifting process.

9.   Make sure the lifting equipment is safe before you start.

10.   Warm-up thoroughly before training.

11.   Engage in regular flexibility exercises at the same time as you work to develop strength.

12.   Try never to stress the same muscle groups in collective exercises.

13.   Never use weights if you know you have a muscular or a joint injury.

14.   Use supportive equipment such as a weights belt when lifting heavy weights.

Remember that soccer players need high levels of dynamic strength for soccer. They may also need maximal strength in any all-out efforts to win a tackle and gain the ball, and muscular endurance when performing sub-maximal work such as continuous running or off-setting fatigue. Thus it is clear that strength training is essential for the soccer player's development.

Speed and power training

Speed and power are very important components in any analysis of human performance. Speed seems to be somewhat unique as a physical fitness component in that it is strongly influenced by innate, hereditary factors and is also bound up with the body's nervous system. Other components of fitness have an effect on speed, most notably strength and flexibility. Similarly, power is best understood as a subcomponent of several other components of physical fitness, that is as an amalgam of strength, speed and flexibility.

In soccer, speed can manifest itself in many different ways. In the frenzied inter-play of action in a game we may witness the following examples:

- a striker's *speed off the mark* in the penalty area
- a goalkeeper's *speed of reaction* (reaction-time) when making a save
- the *limb speed* used in striking or throwing a ball
- the *speed endurance* of the midfield player who is in perpetual motion
- the flat out *maximal speed* of the defender chasing back
- the *explosive speed* involved in diving, twisting and turning.

Clearly then, speed and power are vital to the soccer player and there exist numerous ways to train for these components. In fact, there are many so-called 'proven' methods for training the elusive and yet key ingredient of speed. The individual should be exposed to a wide variety of drills and monitored to see which are the most successful.

Fast reactions and initial speed off the mark are essential qualities for all soccer players, given that they are continually interacting with team-mates and opponents, and responding to on and off-the-ball cues of a physical, visual and verbal nature. If we consider the lack of time and space that an attacker is given by any good defender, or a 10–20 metre (10–21 yard) sprint for the ball in space, then we can understand the value of a fast reaction-time. That initial

'pick-up', which has both a physiological and a psychological base, is often the hallmark of a great player, especially the 'finishers' or the goal-scorers. These players often have superb balance and are very quick over those important first two or three strides. Match analysis statistics show that a soccer game often consists of many short runs of high intensity, and so it is clear that initial speed off the mark is of major importance.

Speed in running is a function of stride frequency and length. Stride frequency is determined by the central nervous system and, to a large extent, is genetically pre-determined. Stride length is affected by the player's ability to apply an effective propulsive force by means of the driving leg in its contact with the ground, and also by his range of movement potential at the hip, the knee and the ankle joints. This latter aspect is of particular importance because it *is* trainable, especially if sprinting drills are used, while the previous point bears testimony to the importance of doing strength and flexibility work. A player's ability to do fast drills like simultaneous high knee-raises and arm pumping, or pitter-patter 'quick heels' up to the buttocks, are initial indications of limb speed.

However, to improve speed the player's running action needs to be analysed. Many critics will say that a footballer should concentrate on ball work because he has to run with the ball at his feet. But if you look at any player's on-the-ball action you will see that many of his contacts are only single touches or last only a few brief seconds, thus demonstrating just how vital are off-the-ball running skills. The player needs to ask himself if he is mechanically efficient in his running. Running speed will improve if the following basic pointers are taken on board.

1. Make a good contact with the ground at a point directly under the upper body.
2. Keep the head relaxed and look forwards.
3. Generate a fast and full arm action and relax the shoulders.
4. Adopt a forward lean in the upper body. Try not to be too upright in your sprinting. Generate a full leg drive and extension; push the ground back behind you.

Before doing any speed training and after a thorough warm-up, it is useful to do a number of simple speed drills. These will help you to develop 'fast feet' because they are positive neuro-muscular readiness activities and open up neural pathways prior to any bout of physical sprint work.

Sprint training

In all speed work the player should attempt to remain in complete control in his running; being relaxed and at ease with a particular running style is vital for psychological and physiological reasons. Believing and feeling that he can be fast is often essential to any sportsman for whom speed is an essential ingredient.

Hollow sprints

This exercise replicates quite nicely the game demands of soccer. A group of players should perform the following schedule for a period of 20–5 minutes, with a continual emphasis on quality work and periods for complete recovery.

Warm-up and stretching

	sprint 40m	sprint 60m
Sprint Set	jog 60m OR	jog 40m
	stride/walk 100m	walk 100m
	repeat through 400m	

Short rest allowing recovery

Acceleration sprints

As the term implies this involves the player engaging in a series of sprints which begin with a steady 'rolling' start, that is they progress from walking to jogging to striding to sprinting in any single repetition. With a walk-back recovery, which allows the player to prepare completely for the next run, this type of training can help build speed and muscular strength. A typical set might involve twelve to fifteen 200 metre 'turn around' acceleration sprints, wherein the player jogs, strides and sprints for 50 metres each before easing down, walking 50 metres and repeating the whole exercise.

   This type of work is particularly good for cold weather because it does not demand explosive starting, but rather a controlled build-up of the running tempo.

Repetition sprints

In this exercise the player does a number of repetitions for specific distances at a pre-determined rate of running (ideally between 80–100% effort). Clearly this work requires complete recovery following each run, and the ideal recovery would be a slow, lengthy jog before returning to the starting position. Jogging and/or active stretching between repetitions will help dissipate the waste products in the working muscles quicker than simple rest/non-activity. The following set is suitable for soccer players:

$$6 \times \quad 15 \text{ m}$$
$$5 \times \quad 25 \text{ m}$$
$$4 \times \quad 35 \text{ m}$$
$$3 \times \quad 40 \text{ m}$$
$$2 \times \quad 80 \text{ m}$$
$$1 \times 100 \text{ m}$$

Other sprint schedules can be designed where a consideration for the type of environment in which the players train has an effect on the work done. For example, running down gentle slopes helps to generate a greater stride length and frequency. This type of sprint work has been called **assisted running** because the player experiences a kind of assistance in developing fast sprint speeds. Assisted running like this is valuable because it seems to aid the co-ordination skills involved in sprinting. Care must be given to choosing a long, gentle and smooth surface for this type of running.

   Using the same slope, the player can also experience **resistance running** through sprint work involving uphill repetitions. This latter sprint routine helps speed development in that it strengthens quadriceps and glutei (thigh and buttock muscles) and, if repeated sufficiently, will stress and improve a player's cardio-respiratory endurance capability. Athletics coaches in the past have used surfaces such as sand-dunes or beaches to do this type of speed endurance work, because running on a surface like sand, or in shallow waters, is excellent for sprint resistance training. Other devices that have been adopted or copied from recent American fitness trends are weighted wristlets and anklets worn while sprinting, and harness resistance running.

Shuttle running

It has to be remembered that as well as good maximal sprint speed soccer players will have to have very high speed endurance levels. One valuable type of speed endurance training is

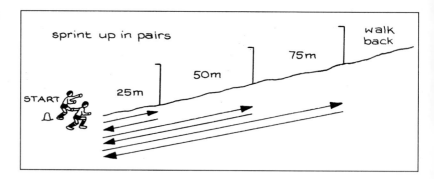

Fig. 119 Shuttle running uphill

sprint up in pairs

walk back

75m

50m

25m

START

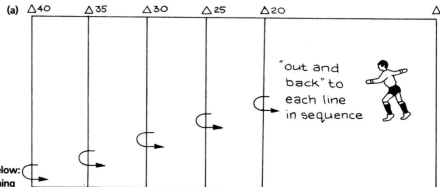

(a) △40 △35 △30 △25 △20 △

"out and back" to each line in sequence

Fig. 120 Right and below: structured shuttle running

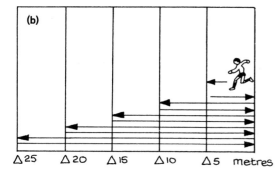

(b)

△25 △20 △15 △10 △5 metres

performing sprint shuttle runs up a slight incline (see fig.119). This work demands a short sprint explosiveness (i.e. high intensity efforts) while allowing for a structured rest (recovery period).

Other types of sprint shuttle running might involve working off specific time and rest intervals over a structured shuttle layout. For example, on the course shown in fig.120a players could sprint in pairs with each player alternately calling 'Go' and working for 45 seconds with 45 seconds' rest, scoring a point for each consecutive line reached in the working period. These very short sprints incorporate multiple fast turns which are vital in developing the high agility demands required of soccer players. Given that footballers rarely have to sprint long distances, another sprint shuttle layout might be an 'out-and-back' set as shown in fig.120(b).

Guidelines for sprint training

Whatever sprint training methods you decide on as a player or a coach, there are a number of important guidelines that need to be stressed.

1. Always emphasise the need for quality sprinting, both physically and technically.
2. Train over the game distance for soccer, i.e. sprinting for 25–40 metres.
3. Occasionally perform sprint work over distance (e.g. 80–100 metres).
4. Allow for proper recovery.
5. Make sure that you have already established a good aerobic base (endurance capacity) so that quality work can be sustained.
6. Always perform an extensive warm-up prior to sprint work and *stay* warm by wearing sufficient loose clothing.
7. Do not arrive at sprint work already tired.

Plyometrics

One type of training that has risen to prominence over the last decade in sports where high levels of speed and explosiveness are required is **plyometrics**. The drills involved in this form of training have been widely used by American Footballers, for whom power as well as sheer strength and speed are of the utmost importance. They have also become an increasingly common part of training for volleyball players and athletes in jumping events. The exercises involve bounding, rebounding and depth-jumping activities.

What the soccer player is trying to develop is, simply speaking, his 'bounce' potential, and he does this through repeated 'active' landings where rapidity of movement during contact time with the ground is essential. Plyometrics attempts to train the eccentric aspect of muscular action, where the muscle lengthens *and* develops maximum tension. If this is followed quickly with a phase of concentric action (as occurs in plyometric work after a 'gathering' phase on landing), then greater amounts of elastic energy can be generated and utilised.

The following are some possible individual plyometric exercises.

1. Repeated two-footed leaping (leap-frog style) for height and distance.

Fig. 121   Plyometrics exercise involving leaping

2. Repeated bounding (for height and some forward movement).

Fig. 122   Plyometrics exercise involving bounding

3. Repeated bounding strides (for controlled distance).

Fig. 123   Plyometrics exercise using bounding strides

A plyometrics circuit for a soccer squad could be constructed in a small gymnasium (see fig.124) and might include some upper body work linked to soccer action, using soccer balls and *small* medicine balls. Each activity is performed for 30 seconds, and is followed by 60 seconds' rest. The player works with a partner and performs 2 complete circuits after a thorough warm-up and stretching routine.

Plyometrics will certainly help develop a footballer's anaerobic power output, which will in turn lead to improvements in speed on the field of play. However, this type of work should only be done when a solid period of all-round fitness training has already been undertaken. Also, only properly designed training/jogging shoes which have good absorption and supportive qualities in the heel and sole should be worn, and the player ought always to engage in a thorough warm-down so as to minimise any localised muscular soreness, especially around the knee joints.

Flexibility training

Many soccer players often ignore, or only pay lip service to, flexibility as an integral aspect of their training. The main reason why every soccer player, irrespective of age or ability, should enter into flexibility work (i.e. stretching exercises), is that it will help reduce the risk of injury if it precedes training or match play. Stretching, therefore, helps prepare the player's body for vigorous activity in that the muscles surrounding a joint complex can be taken through their entire range of movement in readiness to meet

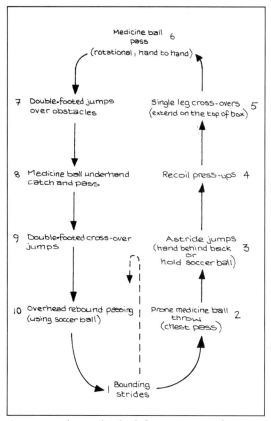

Fig. 124 A plyometrics circuit for a soccer squad

Figure labels:

6 Medicine ball pass (rotational, hand to hand)

7 Double-footed jumps over obstacles

5 Single leg cross-overs (extend on the top of box)

8 Medicine ball underhand catch and pass

4 Recoil press-ups

9 Double-footed cross-over jumps

3 Astride jumps (hand behind back or hold soccer ball)

10 Overhead rebound passing (using soccer ball)

2 Prone medicine ball throw (chest pass)

1 Bounding strides

the demands of the game. Basically, any flexibility regime is searching to increase the range of movement at a joint or joint complex by stretching those muscles involved beyond their habitual length.

Improved flexibility can also aid speed, strength and endurance. If a player develops his joint flexibility (at the ankles, the hips and the shoulders), then the body parts will be able to work over a greater range of movement and thus generate greater force and speed. This improved movement potential may help in the execution of difficult skills, particularly where agility is at a premium (e.g. in goal). Also, when a sound balance is struck in training between muscular strength development and flexibility improvement then no loss in the range of movement around a joint will occur. Hypertrophy (the building of muscle bulk), developed by strength training, will not limit mobility provided that the player follows a comprehensive flexibility routine at the same time. Indeed, we know that a structured involvement with weights and flexibility exercises

in a training regime helps to protect potentially weak joints.

It is important to note that there are two kinds of flexibility.

1. Dynamic flexibility: this relates to those forces which oppose or resist throughout the range of motion of a joint.
2. Static flexibility: this relates to the range of motion about a joint.

The latter type of flexibility is more easily measured, but research has generally concluded that the major forces which resist joint mobility (and are most difficult to measure) are linked to the elasticity of soft tissue (muscle).

We must remember that structurally man is not like most machines in that the latter are designed and manufactured to operate within a fixed, rigid framework provided by many and various immovable joints. The human body searches for rigidity (especially important when the sport is a collision sport like soccer) which is provided through bones (skeleton), muscles, joints, tendons and connective tissue and skin. It also requires suppleness, especially when seeking to apply maximum force through greater ranges of movement (e.g. in soccer, hip mobility enhances the range of kick and the stride in running). Muscles contribute about 40% of the resistance to flexibility in joints. So, if we know that flexibility can be positively altered via the utilisation of stretching regimes, then ranges of joint motion can be improved where necessary.

Ballistic stretching exercises

Two main categories of stretching exercises exist: ballistic and static flexibility. Ballistic stretching exercises are sometimes used by athletes, especially sprinters and throwers. They involve a bouncy, rhythmic movement of limbs, by means of which momentum is built up. Researchers suggest that this work helps maintain the existing range of joint movement, but does not consciously attempt to improve the habitual length of the muscles involved. In fact, the bouncing action only initiates a stretch reflex which triggers a transitory lengthening of the muscle. Strains can develop this way which, in time, might lead to a build-up of scar tissue and subsequent loss of elasticity. So, unless conducted very carefully, ballistic stretching is potentially hazardous and generally is an undesirable training medium for soccer players.

Unfortunately, tradition seems to have dictated that these jerky stretch drills are the most likely to be handed down by ex-professional players as they enter into coaching.

Static flexibility exercises

Static flexibility exercises are by far the most sensible stretching drills. These drills are the reverse of ballistic stretching and involve holding a slow, maintained stretch, so encouraging a muscle lengthening process to occur. There are two types of static stretch. **Active** stretching involves the player completing the stretch on his own initiative and holding each exercise for 15–20 seconds. **Passive** stretching involves the player initiating the stretch, but then being helped in the final part of the stretch by an external force, e.g. another player or the coach.

In passive stretching, the final work in developing movement is *not* being done by a muscle (the prime mover) but by an outside agent, for example a careful partner who listens and stops applying extra force when the player feels any pain. This form of stretching can be very worth while because it focuses on the player in the strech position attempting to relax the antagonist muscle, that is the stressed muscle which he is seeking to lengthen. Also, doing this sort of partner work literally brings players together and puts the responsibility on them as individuals. Indeed, the coach should simply be present at flexibility work as a consultant and an adviser as to the safety elements involved in any stretching routine, having conveyed already to the players the value and nature of the work involved. The following are some specific pieces of information that the coach might pass on.

Guidelines for stretching

1.   Jog for a short period of time before beginning your exercises and make sure that you are suitably clothed. The aim initially is to warm-up and supply the muscles about to be stretched with an increased blood flow. If you begin stretching without doing some jogging and simple callisthenics, then you run the risk of ligamental damage.
2.   Design a stretching routine which you know works for soccer and concentrates particularly on the game's requirements (e.g. your ankle joints will need extra stretching time because of

the repeated knocks they suffer in match play).
3.   Make sure that the routine has a pattern, e.g. head to toe, or large muscle groups to specific joint complexes.
4.   The initial routine of between 10 and 15 individual stretches should last about 5 minutes, with each stretch being held for about 20 seconds.
5.   Do not try to induce pain during any of your stretching, and do not strain to get into any position. You should feel a controlled tension whilst stretching but no more. The 'no pain, no gain' syndrome does not apply here.
6.   Having completed an initial jog, some callisthenics and a period of 5 minutes' general flexibility, you will be ready to begin a full stretching routine.
7.   Each stretched position should be held for 15–20 seconds. After the feeling of tension decreases (in around 10–15 seconds) try and feel a further stretch in the muscle for about 5 seconds and then *gradually* come out of the stretch.
8.   Try to understand what your body is saying to you; if you 'feel' the stretch is near the joint complex then it is likely that you are overworking tendons and ligaments. Remember not to bounce but to feel the stress in the main body of the muscle.
9.   Occasionally try PNF (proprioceptive neuro-muscular facilitation) training. This requires the player to hold a stretched position while performing a 5 second fixed isometric contraction. This process can be repeated 2–3 times for each stretch position.
10.   Do not hold your breath while stretching as this only produces body tension and detracts from any relaxed state you are trying to obtain. You should be aiming to feel relaxed, comfortable and at ease with your body.
11.   More detailed flexibility routines should either be seen as training sessions in their own right (e.g. 30 minutes' quality work-out), or they should be carried out at the end of a hard physical session when all the muscles are thoroughly warmed-up. In this latter situation the stretching exercises act as a physiological and psychological 'cool down' session, reducing muscle soreness and making you think positively about your next physical training session or technical skills work-out.
12.   The frequency of sessions will depend upon the amount of time you have and how serious you are about soccer. Conducting 3 sessions per week, maybe 2 within the general

club sessions and 1 on your own, is not too much to ask.

13. Above all else, try to enjoy these sessions whether you are on your own or with a partner or team of players. Build up a repertoire of stretches which suit you and write them down, commenting on their effectiveness in a training diary.

14. Watch others stretching and learn new ideas.

15. Always attempt to stretch technically correctly.

Active stretching exercises

Neck

1. Adopt a balanced standing position, with your hands on your hips.

2. Drop your head so that your right ear moves to your shoulder and hold it there for a count of 5 before returning your head to an upright position.

3. Let your head drop back and raise your face to the sky. Hold this position for the same count as before, and return to the same position.

4. Let your head drop to your other shoulder and repeat.

5. Let your head drop forwards, with your chin on your chest.

Each of the above movements is held for 5 seconds and the routine is repeated twice. Do not roll or circle your head as this may increase the natural degenerative processes occurring in the invertebral joints of the neck.

Arms and shoulder stretch

1. Stand in a balanced position *or* sit upright with sufficient room around you to work freely.

2. Reach up with your arms and grasp one elbow.

3. Pull down gently on the held elbow so that the free hand moves down between your shoulder-blades.

Hold each position for 10 seconds.

Side-stretch

1. Adopt a balanced standing position, with feet slightly wider than shoulder width apart.

2. Reach with one hand over your head ballet-dancer style, letting the other arm hang free.

3. Bend sideways at the waist and hold that stretching position.

Hold each side-stretch for 10 seconds then relax and repeat the stretch on the other side. Repeat the whole routine twice.

Lower back stretch (1) – trunk stretch

Three lower back stretch exercises are included because of the high incidence of lower back pain in soccer players.

1. Adopt a prone position with the hands shoulder width apart and slightly in front of shoulders.

2. Straighten your arms and at the same time try to push your pelvic girdle down into the ground.

Hold the 'extended' position for 10–15 seconds, relax and then repeat.

Lower back stretch (2) – hamstring stretch

1. Start in a seated position and tuck your knees into your chest.

2. As you bring your knees up, roll backwards and then rock forwards over your spine 3 or 4 times.

3. On the last roll back add extra momentum and finish with your legs straight and your toes held firmly on the floor.

4. Support your lower back with your arms and attempt to push the hips up and back.

5. After the stretch roll out *very* slowly.

Allow 20–30 seconds for each sequence and breathe steadily throughout. Repeat the routine twice.

Hip flexor and buttocks stretch

1. From a supine position, hold one knee with both hands.

2. Pull your knee high up to your chest. Hold this position for 10 seconds.

3. Roll so that your extended leg is still in

contact with the ground and place your bent leg at right angles to the ground.

4. Finally, twist gently back from where you were so as to have your back on the ground, and face upwards with your lower body twisting in the other direction.

5. Hold this position for 10 seconds.

Repeat the routine twice, allowing 20 seconds for each leg.

Groin stretch

1. From a seated position bring the soles of your feet together (held by your hands) and resting your elbows on the insides of your knees.

2. Gently lean forwards, pulling on your feet and simultaneously pressing down on your knees.

Hold the stretch for 10 seconds then relax and repeat.

Hamstring stretch

1. From a seated position place your knees flat against the floor.

2. Keeping a flat back by looking forwards and not downwards, reach along your shins towards your toes. Attempt to hold on to your toes (if you can't, hold on to the underside of your legs), and then hold your calf muscles.

Hold the stretch for 10 seconds, relax and repeat twice more (30 seconds in all).

Quadriceps stretch

1. Stand upright on one leg and raise your free leg so that you can hold your right foot with your right hand. Make sure that you counterbalance this position by working in pairs or against an object such as a wall or a goal-post.

2. Gently pull upwards on the bent foot and simultaneously drive forwards with the bent thigh.

Hold the stretch for 10 seconds, relax and change legs. Repeat twice.

Calf muscle stretch

1. Stand a little distance away from an object which can support your body-weight and (e.g. a wall) offer complete resistance.

2. Support your body-weight against the wall, keeping your arms bent. Bend the lead leg and keep the rear leg straight with its heel firmly on the ground.

3. Let your hips move slowly towards the wall and keep your back flat, feeling the tension in the upper part of your lower leg, that is in the (soleus) calf muscle.

Hold for 10 seconds, relax and change legs. Repeat twice.

Lower calf and Achilles tendon stretch

1. Lean against a wall or a rail (it must be above waist height). The starting position is the same as for the calf stretch, except that the upper body is at a slightly lower angle.

2. Lower your hips and bend slightly at the knees, still keeping your heel down against the ground.

3. Hold the stretch for 10 seconds, relax and change legs. Repeat twice.

Ankle mobilisation and stretch

1. From a seated position, extend one leg and bend the other slightly. Use your arms to support your back.

2. Aim for full plantar flexion (toes pointed forwards) of the foot, followed by foot circling (try writing your first name in the air with your toes!).

3. Next, aim for full dorsi-flexion (toes pointed backwards and upwards) of the foot.

Hold the plantar and dorsi-flexion for 5 seconds each (the whole routine lasts 15 seconds). Relax then change legs. Repeat twice.

Passive stretching exercises

Arm and shoulder stretch

Support your seated partner by placing your

lower leg against his back. Push forwards into his back and pull backwards against his wrists.

Lower back and hamstring stretch

Apply force gently against the shoulder blades when the seated partner desires it. Hold and apply greater force whenever requested so as to increase the stretch.

Trunk and side rotation

A player lies in a supine position with one leg at right angles to the other, his arms outstretched above his head, and his back flat against the floor. His partner directs force gently downwards on to his horizontal leg and his opposite shoulder and forearm.

Calf stretch

One player leans forward against the other, as in the soleus stretch against a solid object. The player 'allowing' a maximal stretch simply steps back, thus generating a greater degree of forward lean in the body position of the player doing the stretching.

Thigh stretch

The player doing the stretching simply holds on to a solid object at around waist height. He drops his upper body forwards (rather like a shot putter at the start of his put) and raises one leg backwards into a 'T' position. The player applying the force simply holds the knee, raising it gently while resting his free arm on his partner's back.

Extra passive stretches using partners can be simply created. Goalkeepers in particular benefit from this type of work because they often train with other goalkeepers or specialist coaches for long periods, and because shoulder strength and mobility are vitally important to them.

NUTRITION AND DIET

For physical work to occur we know that force must be generated and applied. This is brought about by multiple muscular contractions which in turn require an energy source—food. However, generally speaking we do not pay enough attention to what we eat, especially when 'eating for sport'. Soccer players in particular are notorious for their poor approach to diet.

Nutrition and soccer performance

It would be nice to think that one single food source could supply us with all our nutritional requirements. However, human beings require a balanced and varied intake of food to provide them with all the essential nutrients. The nutrients that help maintain good health are as follows:

- carbohydrates
- proteins
- fats
- minerals
- vitamins
- fibre
- water.

Soccer players should try to find out more about the structure, source and function of the major nutrients and take an active interest in the nature and quality of their diet (see, for example, *Diet in Sport* by Wilf Paish, A & C Black, 1989). Nutritionists and sports scientists agree that players' diets should be high in carbohydrate and low in fat, particularly animal fats. Care should be taken to ensure that carbohydrate intake is rich in nutrients and also that only an average quantity of protein is consumed. Sportsmen often concentrate on having extra protein in their diet at the expense of a satisfactory fibre intake. Fibre is the non-digestible, bulky (stalks and outer layer) section of plant food that facilitates the proper functioning of the bowel and helps prevent constipation and other related diseases.

Finally, we need to dispel some of the myths surrounding nutrition. Many soccer players like to have a drink and believe that a little tipple before a game helps their performance. Alcohol is largely fermented carbohydrate (50% sugars and starches), but cannot be used like other carbohydrates to provide energy during exercise because it metabolises in the liver at a slow rate. Excess alcohol simply provides an energy source which is stored as fat (non-productive weight), and it can have a detrimental effect on the liver. It is far more important to take in a regular supply of water during training and on match day, since an inadequate water intake has a quick and serious debilitating effect on performance.

Another myth is that extra doses of vitamins improve performance. On the contrary, ingesting some vitamins in large quantities only leads to joint pain, headaches and fatigue caused by toxicity.

Energy systems

The digestive system synthesises food into fats and sugars, thus supplying the 'energy' which is used to help manufacture adenosine triphosphate (ATP). ATP is a chemical compound which, when broken down into adenosine diphosphate (ADP), provides the energy fuel for muscles to work. The generation of ATP is also linked to how long muscles can work for. The aerobic system utilises three fuels – fats, carbohydrates and proteins (amino acids), while the anaerobic system uses only glucose from carbohydrates when producing an energy source. Also, the aerobic system deals easily with the end-products of its metabolic process while the anaerobic system cannot cope with the large quantities of lactic acid left in the blood and the muscles, thus resulting in fatigue. As has been said before, soccer is a game which has a predominantly aerobic nature, with bouts of anaerobic work interspersed within it, such that carbohydrate and glycogen stores are being depleted every time a player trains or takes part in a match. The key factor is to refill that energy

reservoir by eating the most beneficial foods, and thus good eating habits are clearly vital to the soccer player.

Diet for soccer training

It would be wrong to think that we could or should prescribe an ideal diet for a soccer player in training. For a start there are a number of variables, such as the size and the age of the player, environmental (humidity and heat) factors and personal preferences, which prevent us from designing a 'standard' player's diet. Research has recommended the following basic guidelines:

- eat less fat, particularly animal fats
- increase dietary fibre intake
- reduce sugar consumption
- reduce salt intake.

Calorific intake is also vital. For the average young male approximately 2,800–3,000 kilo-calories per day (12.6 megajoules) would be sufficient. However, for a professional soccer player that would rise to 5,000–6,000 kilo-calories per day (20 megajoules). Also, it is worth noting that youngsters between 12 and 20 years of age will require extra energy for periods of rapid growth as well as for physical activity.

Thus a professional soccer player would need to have a diet which was approximately 50% carbohydrate (preferably complex carbohydrates) and 15% protein, or in calorific terms:

Carbohydrate: 2,800 k.cal.
Protein: 750 k.cal.
Fat: 1,450 k.cal.

A very active soccer player will need to have 3 or 4 meal-times a day with nutritious snacks in between at appropriate moments. These snacks, which would be taken ideally after a morning training session, might include wholegrain sandwiches, nuts, fruit, biscuits, muesli bars or a fizzy drink. Research has suggested that consuming liquid a few minutes after strenuous exercise is very beneficial, in that it stabilises blood glucose levels. This sort of 'snack' supplement would also be suitable for the mid-afternoon if training is in the evening. Post-training, the main meal could then be consumed at around 8.30 p.m. Basically, the main thing to remember is to re-stock fuel reserves with the right nutrients at the right time, that is around training time.

Match-day diet

Match-day meals have a symbolic importance because they bring the team and the management together. Thus, on this day we have to consider psychological as well as nutritional factors. The following are some useful guidelines.

1. Avoid eating fats and large amounts of meat because they require lengthy digestive periods and hinder stomach emptying, creating a feeling of fullness and heaviness.
2. Avoid greasy foods which form gas.
3. Eat lots of complex carbohydrates with a high calorie content because these are easily digested. Avoid eating excessive amounts of simple carbohydrates.
4. Ensure that any meal is consumed at least $2\frac{1}{2}$–4 hours before kick-off time.

A major psychological factor will be the close proximity of the big match and the consequent emotional pressures and tensions on the individual, and indigestion or an inability to eat a solid meal may result. Liquid pre-match meal substitutes are increasingly popular in certain individual and team sports because these types of balanced meal (i.e. mixtures of large proportions of carbohydrate plus protein and fat) can reduce nervous indigestion, nausea, vomiting and abdominal cramps, and they are also satisfying and tasty. But above all else the important thing is that they are digested simply and remove the need for a liquefaction process in the stomach under anxiety situations.

Diet *during* play is also important in soccer, especially if the game is played in heat and goes into extra time. Insufficient fluid intake during competition will affect your ability to lose body heat through sweating, and may result in heat-stroke. Ideally, a soccer player should sip fluid intermittently (some physiotherapists have fluid sachets or bottles readily available for players when they come on to treat an injury), but if the only opportunity for a drink is at half-time then an electrolyte/glucose fluid solution (e.g. Lucozade) or good old water is essential.

Diet post-activity

Following a match or a training session (especially during endurance work-outs) every attempt should be made to replace the carbohydrates, proteins, fats, minerals, vitamins and water lost. In effect, given the continuous cycle of training, match preparation and game that is soccer, a player's body constantly has to re-stock its energy stores, that is its muscle and liver glycogen levels. Research has shown that sustaining a high carbohydrate diet will allow for complete glycogen re-synthesis within 48 hours, whereas a protein and fat diet will only offer partial glycogen replenishment after 4 days of recovery.

THE PSYCHOLOGICAL REQUIREMENTS OF THE GAME

A player who is able to motivate himself positively for competition helps not only himself but also his team. In soccer we devote a lot of time to preparing players and teams for the physical demands of the game and the fine nuances of tactical appreciation that are necessary to create success. However, we rarely even consider, let alone plan for, any psychological factors. Yet as players' levels of physical and tactical preparation improve and ultimately cancel each other out, sports psychology will come to hold the key to success in soccer. All too often psychological preparation is left to the coach and/or team captain to deal with in a pre-match talk which aims to create a blanket readiness by addressing all the players at once. Clearly this will suit some, but not all players, and one set format will not be adequate for a whole season.

The following are a number of important psychological factors which need explaining. For a more detailed analysis of sports psychology read Willi Railo's excellent book *Willing to Win* (Springfield Books) or John Syer and Chris Conolly's guide to mental training *Sporting Body, Sporting Mind* (Cambridge University Press).

Arousal

This term describes the degree of alertness or attentiveness displayed by a player prior to and during competition. Arousal is linked to tension and emotional excitement, and it may be induced by increased motivation or aggressive behaviour by the player himself or by others, or it may be enhanced by external stimuli such as the roar of the crowd. It is widely believed by sports psychologists and exercise physiologists that an organised bout of vigorous physical activity (lasting around 5–10 minutes) is the simplest way of arousing a team for competition. A number of top English First Division clubs are now well versed in pre-match warm-up and post match warm-down routines of a physical *and* a psychological nature.

Stress

Stress is a psycho-physiological response to any influence which upsets the homeostasis (inner balance) of a player. An important game could bring nervousness and fear of not performing as well as one could. Those nerves can bring on tension and anxiety, resulting, for example, in a loss of composure in the performance of a normally assured player. Nervous behaviour in any soccer player is an example of a stress reaction. However, this behaviour is usually only the result of the player preparing himself for a supreme physical effort, and it is not necessarily a bad thing provided that the internal stresses can be channelled positively.

Stress also may be caused by such factors as the quality of the opposition, the weather, the playing surface, the stadium, the mood of the spectators, the temperament of the referee and possibly the composition of your own team.

These are just a few of the variables which can impinge on performance if you, as a player or as a coach, allow it!

Anxiety

The biggest cause of stress may in fact be the player's own, or other peoples' (team-mates, officials, parents) desire to succeed, because if that objective is not achieved the player will experience anxiety. In a team game like football there can only be one winner and one loser (apart from drawn games!) from a match, and in the course of a season there will be far more losers than winners. Yet individual and collective progress is still measured in terms of matches won, drawn or lost instead of according to individual rates of progress based on factors such as skill improvement, physical conditioning and psychological readiness. Surely one of the main reasons why any player engages in competitive soccer is his desire to improve his performance and skill levels. Inhibitions will mount if pressure is put on him to cultivate an overriding desire for victory. Very few players have this strong desire for victory without also being afraid to fail. The secret is perhaps for players to set themselves realistic performance targets, and for coaches and managers to be sympathetic and understanding about defeats. Failure to succeed is more than punishment enough for any player! The important thing is to learn from that experience.

Reactions to stressful situations in soccer are generally two-fold, with the player responding either with inhibition or fear, as has been described, or with anger and aggression.

Aggression

This reaction normally occurs in soccer players when they are unable to handle a situation in the proper manner. For example, if a player loses the ball in a fair but hard tackle, he may respond by fouling his opponent. Soccer administrators and officials would probably say that promoting aggression in soccer players is ethically and morally indefensible.

However, given that the modern game is highly competitive, it is not difficult to see why players, coaches and managers pander to this aggressive instinct in man's nature. Therefore, it would seem useful to distinguish between instrumental aggression, which is positive, and destructive aggression, which is purely negative.

Many coaches and the media condone aggressive play, arguing that it signifies a willingness on the part of the players to fight hard for victory. Players themselves seem to tolerate provocation, threats and foul play as being 'part of the game'. It is only actions which bring a real threat of injury that are now deemed to be aggressive. This is a sad state of affairs but seems to be an inevitable consequence or by-product of the fact that the 'prizes' at stake in the game are so valuable. However, given that soccer stars appear regularly on television and are seen and copied by countless millions of youngsters, they should offer up an acceptable image of themselves and their game. One very practical way of dealing with aggressive behaviour is to focus the attack on the ball and not the player.

Motivation

Motivation is a factor which is present both *in* the individual player and *between* groups of players. Thus there is motivation both of the goal-oriented nature and of the type built on a bond between team-mates.

Motivation is transient and ever-changing. One means of sustaining motivation might be to treat each player as an individual, so that his desires and emotional needs are met in a sharing and concerned way. Alternatively, the manager can lead his team in an autocratic, authoritarian manner.

It is important to remember that motivation is personal and that the most successful soccer players are those who can mature into self-motivating individuals. External targets are important in soccer but players may also choose to participate for fun, skill development and personal recognition. The motivational desires and needs of a team and of individual players may be fulfilled by constantly communicating, building trust and creating an openness and freedom which fosters a total well-being.

Security

Security comes when a player feels accepted into the team, by his coach, and (with professional players) by his fans. A soccer club is, or should be, just like an extended family, providing social bonding and a familiar, secure environment for its players. Team-mates and the soccer club in general must offer the security which players search for. This security is fundamental to self-confidence, and all soccer players need that quality in abundance.

Confidence

In soccer, there is possibly no other single factor as important as confidence. When a player is self-confident he will perform at his best but it is also important that others believe in him as well. It is dangerous to build your confidence totally around performance, because if your play begins to suffer then so will your mood. The essential ingredient in building self-confidence is emotional control, that is coping well when the pressure is on. The sports psychologist Willi Railo advocates a control imagery, whereby a player who is faced with a big match, noisy spectators or a strange environment consciously thinks of a 'control room' to which he can retire. Once inside this 'room' the player is in charge and untouchable; he becomes in essence all-powerful and can act positively in his soccer performance. What is happening psychologically is that the player shuts out all disruptions and hones in on the act of performing. Repeating over and over again a positive phrase such as 'I am master of this ball' may also help.

Concentration

Concentration in soccer is vital both on and off the ball, allowing the player to direct his thoughts well. When a player is concentrating fully he is in essence preparing himself mentally for the match.

Sports psychologists would say that there are countless other impulses, desires and emotions that we need to experience in our 'readiness' to play soccer, for example courage, enjoyment, risk, affiliation, commitment and trust. In this chapter I have highlighted what I think are the major psychological factors affecting performance. In the next chapter some types of mental strategy that will encourage positive thinking and help soccer players in their psychological training are outlined.

MENTAL TRAINING

Soccer coaches and players spend long hours in physical training and technical practices, yet they tend to ignore any training of the mind for soccer performance. This is possibly because the psychological side of preparation for competition is understood by too few players and coaches. Some managers and players intuitively get it right, or hit on an approach which seems to work, but not many of them give any structured attention to the mental skills which can be enhanced through training and which, therefore, have a positive effect on playing performance.

Some of the factors which need to be attended to have been commented on briefly already, for example confidence, concentration, motivation and anxiety. The following are some initial control mechanisms for coaches and players which, if used properly, will increase their chances of achieving the desired levels of success in soccer. Of course the mental skills which are learned go beyond the game, and become life skills which will help enhance self-image and self-esteem.

Goal-setting

The most central of all mental training skills is the setting of realistic and worth-while targets. These can be decided objectively between the coach and the player and they involve the clear identification of goals before the start of any new training programme or competitive season. What needs to happen is that teams talk collectively with their coaches and decide on a number of short-term and long-term objectives for the new season. Once these are agreed it may be sufficient just to inform each player by posting them publicly in the dressing room, or writing a 'letter of intent' for the coming season. Remember that these goals have to be attainable and that the players have to feel that this is the case. In addition an individual player may sit down on his own and write down a series of long-term and short-term objectives that he would wish to achieve from his involvement in soccer, for example:

ultimate goals: to play for England and win 50 caps
seasonal goals: to help win promotion to Division 2
monthly goals: to win at least one away-match
match goals: to create a scoring opportunity.

The player might list a number of objectives for each of these categories. After listing them the player should file them somewhere and then return to the lists a day or two later to re-appraise them, ranking those which are most important. The player might also write down a series of 'stages' (which may be time-bounded) whereby he can monitor his progress towards goal attainment. At the same time he also is helping himself to map out a clear programme for both mental and physical training.

Mental rehearsal

If achievable goals are set then the psychological effect is one of increased confidence. By having a number of realistic, attainable short-term goals and obtaining them, a player will develop a strong sense of self-belief. It has been said that this leads to confident 'imagining' and results in players making clear, positive statements to themselves about their ability to perform certain soccer skills. Thus this is a form of mental rehearsal, whereby a player visually thinks through a future movement or action, or recalls a moment when he performed brilliantly, in order that he can create positive images immediately prior to competition. Research has shown that mental rehearsal can help speed up the learning process in sports skill development.

Learning how to visualise takes time, as with any skill. The technique can be performed alone, or it can be coach-led. Often soccer coaches will not have the time to promote this type of skill development, and so a sports psychologist may have to be brought in. Working on your own, you should start by simply finding time to sit down (not lying down because you might pop off to sleep!) and relax for a few minutes at a set time each day. Then, just try concentrating on a visual image of yourself or of the player you admire most in a previous good performance. What you are doing is 'seeing' and experiencing in your mind a high level performance, and enjoying that visual and kinaesthetic sensation. It helps if you concentrate on a particular aspect of play, for example an approach and successful strike at goal, so that you recall information which helps build an inter-relationship between mental and physical skills practices. Some sportperformers visualise best by imagining they are a second self, watching their own performance close by the action. In that way they see, hear and feel the movement, and present a clear self-image to themselves.

Another practice involves sitting somewhere where you know you won't be disturbed, and creating in your mind an environment where you are playing or training. Thus you see a sort of clip of the action and view the sequence from many angles, watching for as many good points as possible. In time you will be able, like the cameraman, to focus in on minute detail in order to feel and break down the movement. Finally, you should return to the whole skill and the environment in which it takes place, before ending the visualisation session.

Relaxation

Visualisation or 'imagining' exercises can also be performed by engaging in relaxation techniques. Relaxation in soccer is important because players at all levels need to be able to relax temporarily or totally from the rigours of competition. At times soccer players will need to get away from the pressures of an impending big match and channel their emotions and actions in other directions, perhaps by playing another sport which gives them pleasure without pressure.

Other strategies involve being able to reduce arousal levels immediately prior to and during competition in order to retain a sense of psychological balance and control. The most natural relaxation technique is deep breathing which, psychologically and physiologically, should help a player to relax. Other methods include massage, warm baths and/or an active warm-up, which all reduce muscular tension and, therefore, lower levels of stress. Some sportsmen actively contract and relax certain muscle groups which they know they will use a

lot in a game. Others have clear symbols in their mind and sometimes repeat key words to themselves to evoke feelings of strength and advocate a positive mentality. Another approach relates to the development of self-control using concentration and deep relaxation. The individual concentrates on relaxing every part of the body until a total relaxation occurs.

Built into these relaxation techniques is the need to concentrate totally on the exercise, which is invaluable for a sport like soccer where concentration is essential. Simple concentration exercises might involve a player visualising his own skill execution and honing in on a particular part of the skill (e.g. contact with the ball in a pass).

Mental preparation

What should occur during this process is a focusing of body and mind for action. Soccer players regularly go through a structured routine for physical preparation, but they rarely undertake any mental preparation that could be called structured or organised. This is, however, quite easily done, and should start with the player getting himself in the right mood by tuning in to the stadium and to the general environment where the match will take place. Playing away, particularly on unfamiliar territory, can be disconcerting and rival fans, the state of the pitch and the changing room facilities are all factors which can distract a visiting team. However, by arriving early and absorbing the atmosphere (e.g. by walking the pitch as a team) players can learn to come to terms with their playing environment.

Prior to changing, or early on as you change in readiness for a match, you should take time out by sitting down and actually 'taking in' exactly where you are. A quiet moment, reflecting on your self and your surroundings before facing the hubbub on the pitch, is invaluable. In the final 5–10 minutes before kick-off when the team is ready to go out, there is much to be said for paying attention to the needs of your team-mates, sharing concerns, talking key points through together, and reminding each other of points raised in an earlier team talk. Different units such as the central defenders, the strikers, the midfield trio, and the wide defenders and the goalkeeper might get together so that a positive feeling of team spirit develops. Drawing on particular sources such as the captain, the coach or any player who vocalises feelings in a sensitive and confident manner is also useful, particularly if this becomes something of a ritual that instills a feeling of collective strength and team bonding. An acute awareness of the self and the team should be fostered, and a singular focus should emerge with respect to the team's purpose in the match. A final mental task for each player to perform would be to recall visually (and possibly verbally to himself) those specific tasks to which he has been entrusted. Then, and only then is the soccer player totally ready for the 'big match' and a quality performance.

SAFETY AND INJURY PREVENTION

Every soccer player should be allowed to play and train in the safest possible sporting environment, therefore all players and officials should have an overt concern for safety in soccer and make every attempt to minimise the risk of injury. Initially, each player should be asked to provide a detailed breakdown of his state of health to a club coach or physician. It is advisable that a 'history' of the player's health (i.e. both his previous general health *and* his sport specific injuries) is made known to club officials before he is allowed to embark on any strenuous training programme. Once this medical check has been made and passed satisfactorily, then the soccer player can undergo physical conditioning which is specific to the demands of soccer, and to his particular playing position.

Soccer coaches might draw up simple testing or screening procedures (e.g. a 600 metre timed run, a certain no. of sit ups or press-ups in 1 minute etc.) in order to gather data on the performance of potential players, and set levels of fitness which will be necessary for access into match situations. Clearly no player should be allowed to compete in a game if he cannot be expected to last the whole match. If a player fatigues when the demands placed upon him are not excessive, then it is likely that he is an injury risk. Therefore, a soccer coach must make sure that specific conditioning for soccer takes place.

Because soccer is a sport mainly concerned with running, kicking and tackling, the lower limbs suffer injuries most frequently. The knee is very vulnerable in tackle situations and ligamental sprains and cartilage tears are most common. Fractures do arise, particularly to the fibula or tibia, but generally the most common injuries are contusions, particularly deep bruising to the quadriceps and other large muscle groups where contact is likely. Goalkeepers receive sprains and dislocations especially to the fingers and the shoulders. As mentioned earlier, over-use injuries are possible in soccer, and in professional soccer tendonitis (notably Achilles tendonitis) is the most common ailment. This is a prime example of an injury caused by lack of flexibility training and proper cool-down exercises after training and match play. Also, the poor ergonomic design of soccer boots leads to bursitis by external friction on the Achilles tendon. Nowadays leading training-shoe designers have removed this heel counter and hopefully soccer boot design will follow this lead.

Generally, at least 80% of all soccer injuries are connected to 'soft tissue' injury. Blisters from new boots, cuts, pulled muscles, torn ligaments and different types of bruising are the order of the day for active soccer players. As mentioned earlier, a player should not be allowed back into action too quickly. Recurrent sprains can permanently weaken ligaments and damage nerve endings. If nerve endings are damaged too much they will not be able to properly monitor the degree of stability within joints. Going back too early to play will only aggravate the injury further in the long term. When the player does return to action the muscles around the weakened joint should be stronger than before in order to help stabilise the joint. Using protective strapping is beneficial provided that it is applied properly by a player or a physiotherapist with a background in sports medicine.

Finally, it is worth mentioning that injury prevention in soccer can be controlled by proper coaching and supervision. Good planning, care and attention to training sessions and match selection will help eliminate many soccer injuries.

Overtraining

Overtraining can result in physical and mental illness, with symptoms such as loss of appetite, tiredness or recurring minor ailments. Players should make sure that the intensity of exercise is varied and balanced with periods of relaxation.

Young footballers

Coaches must not risk skeletal injury that might result in permanent damage by asking too much of young footballers. The growing ends of bones are vulnerable to injury from excessive loading either in resistance exercises or in hard, contact situations. Therefore, coaches must guard against placing young players in potentially harmful situations. Prolonged running on hard surfaces, plyometric exercises and simply too much football, may be examples of the types of training and competition that will bring about injury.

Many youngsters are thrust into Saturday morning league football when they lack the basic skills or are psychologically unprepared for the pressures of competition. Young footballers who have not been properly schooled in the skills of soccer, particularly the contact skills of tackling and challenging for a ball, run the risk of serious injury. Also, junior soccer may pit youngsters of the same age against each other despite the fact that one may be far more physically mature than the other. One means of avoiding this physical imbalance might be to turn to weight rather than age categories.

First aid

The following are some essential items which should be included in a first-aid kit:

- sterile dressings (gauze) for wounds or abrasions
- sticking plasters for minor cuts
- adhesive tape and bandages (crêpe), 3 in., 6 in. and triangular
- antiseptic creams and solutions
- eye-wash sachets
- ice packs or chemical cold packs
- double-sided sticky wrap/bandage
- scissors and safety pins
- antiseptic soap, swabs, hydrogen peroxide (for cleansing)
- aspirin
- list of major accident and emergency telephone numbers
- addresses of club players if contact is necessary.

Coaches or adults supervising a soccer team should follow the guidelines set out below when dealing with an injury.

- Stay calm and reassure the injured player.
- Look at the injured player and assess his injury.
- Listen to the injured player to find out exactly what happened.
- Ask the player to very gently move the injured part, if appropriate.
- Examine and touch the injured limb, head or part of the body.
- Treat the injury if possible.
- Make a decision as to whether the player can carry on, or is in need of expert medical care.

When simple injuries do arise the coach can remember the correct procedure by means of the following mnemonic:

R – rest the injury
I – ice should be applied early to the injury
C – compression bandage should follow
E – elevation.

These procedures will help stop bleeding and will promote a speedy recovery in the damaged tissues. If ice is applied then some type of protection for the skin is advisable (e.g. a towel or grease). Ice should be left on for only 3 minutes in any half-hour application. Subsequently, the injured limb should be bandaged, rested and elevated wherever possible. After 3 days slight exercise can begin, and complete recovery ought to take 7–10 days. Coaches must *not* allow players to train thoroughly or play in matches unless the following criteria have been met:

- 100% range of motion has been returned to injured limb
- 100% strength has returned
- there is no pain resulting from activity
- the player is psychologically ready for action.

Equipment

Many injuries could be prevented if players and coaches were simply to take a number of basic precautions. For example, it is easy to check that the equipment players use is in a good state of repair, is suitable and fits! Having equipment 'parades' or spot-checks (which might include small token fines) is worth while as it encourages players to be knowledgeable in the care and maintenance of their soccer kit and to have pride in their team identity. Coaches should be able to advise young players on their choice of boot, and he should be aware of boot inserts such as sorbothane which help provide a heel or arch support for the foot. Shirts made from man-made fibres should be avoided because they are not good at absorbing moisture (sweat), and this will cause rubbing and rashes which are very uncomfortable.

The ground

It is advisable always to check the pitch or the training ground prior to play. Looking for hazards such as stones or glass only takes a few minutes but it can prevent appalling injuries. Particular care should be taken when playing on artificial surfaces because they can cause nasty friction burns and abrasions unless players wear track-suit trousers or similar protective clothing. Also, specialist footwear exists for these surfaces, which will need to be worn if ankle injuries are to be avoided.

INDEX